MW01288796

Becoming Aphrodite

Becoming Aphrodite

How one question and a mythical goddess led
me to genuine self-love.

Lorrie Gray

Copyright © 2018 Ash Born, Inc

All rights reserved, including the right to reproduce this book or portions thereof in any form whatsoever.

ISBN 9781687043023

Visit the author's website at:

www.lorriegray.com

Cover design by Christopher Gray
Cover illustration by Zoe Gray

Dedication

To Zoe and Nadia.
You were my Why.

Table of Contents

Part 1: Forming the Plan

Chapter 1

The Old Demons Awaken

January 7, 2016

Christmas break was always fun, but getting the kids back in the swing of homeschool had always been...er...un-fun. So in January 2016, my husband, Chris, and I wanted to kick the year off with a field trip. We decided to check out the Getty, which we had been wanting to try out for months. For those outside Los Angeles, the Getty is actually the J. Paul Getty Museum, an art museum with pieces ranging from the Middle Ages to the present. The building itself is a work of art with stark, sleek, modern elements contrasting rugged, beige travertine stones. There are open spaces throughout the grounds scattered with sculptures and water features. The outdoor gardens were, unfortunately, closed during our visit.

We entered the building and stopped for a while in the entrance hall before ever reaching the museum proper just to take in the space. It is a rounded, open room several stories tall with exterior glass walls and a circular skylight that flood it with natural light. The whole place is an architectural masterpiece and we were immediately glad we came.

My daughters, 6 and 9 at the time, really loved drawing and art projects, especially my eldest, Zoe. She was a budding artist, showing both interest and talent, so this seemed like something she would really enjoy. My youngest, Nadia, was mostly excited to not have to do math—even though she's a whiz. Honestly, they may have been just as excited to go grocery shopping. Anything to avoid schoolwork! Still, I could clearly see they were enjoying themselves. They would enter a room with wide-eyed wonder, then give me a big smile before flitting off to take a closer look at the exhibits.

From the outside, my family looked great. Picturesque even. It was not uncommon for strangers to stop us and mention what a "good looking family" we were. (Yes, people actually do that. It's a thing.) If you watched us for any length of time, you would have seen meaningful conversations about art, genuine smiles, and heartfelt laughter. We had such a great time exploring the museum, meandering from room to room. There was no agenda. The kids led, so we played around in some galleries for a while, in others, we barely glanced.

More than once we stopped to simply be grateful for my ability to make the trip out. You see, only a year prior, if I had wanted to spend the day at the Getty, I would have done it from my wheelchair.

I was a smidge handicapped.

I have a genetic condition called Ehlers Danlos Syndrome, a connective tissue disorder. I have a specific type that affects my joints, causing them to be hyper-mobile and dislocate easily.

Looking back, I can see evidence of it during my childhood— extreme flexibility, odd pains, easily bruised skin, and even dislocations—but it was never enough to cause alarm. Some bodies do weird things. Lots of people have "trick knees" or "double jointed elbows" so I didn't think much about the seemingly random symptoms. My first pregnancy was normal, though I did have some unresolved damage to my pelvic floor due to a difficult delivery. My second pregnancy was not so normal. About half-way through, my pelvis became unstable, making walking or sitting painful. Then the bones separated, making walking, sitting, and pretty much everything else nearly impossible. I spent the last half of my pregnancy in bed, on my side, with my legs tied together at the knees to minimize movement. I delivered via C-Section and began *what I thought was* the road to recovery after *what I thought was* a pregnancy-related condition.

The first several months postpartum were also spent in bed before moving on to some very slow and gradual physical therapy. Nine months postpartum, when I should have been fully recovered, it became clear something was wrong. My pelvis still wasn't stable and I had started dislocating other joints as well. Lots of them. My spine became so hyper-mobile that the stress fractured one of the vertebrae in my lower back. I spent the majority of my days in bed in high levels of physical pain, not to mention the emotional pain of not being able to care for my family or even hold my precious new baby, Nadia.

It took years of doctors and specialists before I finally got the diagnosis of Ehlers Danlos Syndrome, a condition that is both permanent and degenerative. Then it was more years of new doctors, more specialists, painful treatment, heavy medications, experimental procedures, physical therapists, and draining our finances dry to try to get me better. If I wasn't at an appointment, I was mostly in bed. That was my life. For FIVE years.

Then, one day, I looked at the outcome of all the treatments Western Medicine had offered me and realized, *this isn't working.* I had done everything that was asked of me. I did every exercise and took every medication and I was getting worse—developing new issues like adrenal fatigue, fibromyalgia, and chronic fatigue syndrome. I decided that there had to be another way.

I began doing my own research. I learned about the human body, the effects of food and stress, natural alternatives to harsh medications, and much more. I tried it all. There wasn't a miracle—a touched by God moment. There was a lot of trial and error. I worked hard every day, month after month, applying everything I learned, and slowly, gradually, I began to improve.

That day at the Getty, I had been wheelchair free for 13 months. I was still learning how to manage my condition. Still improving. I wasn't yet 100%, not by a long shot. I likely never would be, but I was better than I had ever dared to imagine. The fact that I could spend the day exploring a museum *on foot*, even if I would need a couple of days to recover afterwards, made me count my blessings. And they were many. My marriage: tested, but strengthened. My girls: beautiful, inside and out. The future: full of hope. Life was good. I was genuinely thankful. As we walked through the museum, my husband and I both stopped more than once to marvel at my improvement and really soak it in. Sometimes I would catch him just watching me and our girls and smiling.

That should have been enough.

That should have been everything.

For the rest of my life and forevermore I shouldn't have ever complained or been sad about anything else. I could walk when I hadn't been able to walk so now everything should be great, right? I felt like I wasn't allowed to struggle with anything else ever again. I had battled for my health and won.

Now, it was over and it was time to move on to the happily ever after part. That was the general message I got from others as well. My family and friends had been so sad about my condition and so focused on me getting out of my wheelchair that, once I was out, they were like, "Yay! You did it. Aren't you glad all the hard stuff is behind you?" If my body had been the only thing that was broken, perhaps that would have been the case.

Despite my best efforts, guilting myself and giving myself stern lectures about how I had no right to be anything but grateful was making no difference in the reality of my situation. In truth, I was really struggling. It was nothing so obvious as a wheelchair. This struggle was internal and invisible, but just as real. It was also familiar. Years had passed since the last major conflict, but the war had never really ended. I was picking up right where I had left off. Each day was more of a struggle. I was resisting. I was fighting as best I could. I was handling the small skirmishes that broke out, but I could see all-out warfare was coming. It was inevitable, and, this time, I wasn't sure I could win.

Museums have a lot of visual stimulus to hold a person's attention. As long as I was focused on the art, or conversing with my family, things were fine. Unfortunately, as my eyes wandered around the galleries, my mind kept wandering too, straight to negative, obsessive, and cyclical Thoughts about my body—about myself: *I'm ugly. I'm fat. I'm disgusting. I ate too much this morning. I'm going to gain weight. I don't deserve to ever eat food again. I need to not eat the rest of the day. Or tomorrow. I just need to stop eating altogether. If I could just lose this extra weight, everything would be fine. I'll never be good enough. I hate this. I hate my body. Haven't I dealt with enough? This isn't fair.*

14

As we walked around the galleries, I felt my eyes and focus continually being pulled away from the art and onto the other women in the museum. I was so distracted by the comparisons. If they were thinner: self-loathing. If they were bigger: less self-loathing. The reprieve only lasted a moment though, because even if I could feel better about being thinner, I was still stuck with a body that was BROKEN. Getty attendance was high that day, so I had lots of chances for comparison. I was up and down emotionally all day—but mostly down. Realizing I was down made me feel even *more* down. I should have been grateful that I could walk. I should have been having a great time at the museum with my family. Yet I kept finding myself thinking about the size and shape of my body and how much I wished it was different.

When I wasn't comparing body sizes, I was fixated on food. *What have I eaten so far today? Three hundred calories here. Seventy calories there. How are my macros? No more carbs before dinner. Need twenty more grams of protein. WHEN IS LUNCH!?* As we walked around I was continually pulled away from what I was doing with hunger pangs. As usual, I had eaten a small breakfast, stopping before I was really satisfied, and now I was *so* hungry. I kept checking my watch to see when I would be allowed to eat, but not feeling like I could eat anything yet. If I ate lunch too early I might require a snack before dinner, which would increase my overall calories, and that would simply not do. It was better to be uncomfortable now. While I waited, I thought about what food I had packed and meticulously planned out what I would allow myself to eat based on how much food I thought I could consume without gaining weight. It wasn't much. *Better eat it slowly.*

I thought about food constantly. I was obsessed. Totally infatuated. Food. Food. Food. Eating it. Thinking about eating it. Thinking of all the reasons I shouldn't be eating it. Beating myself up after I ate it. Coming up with plans for restricting it.

Researching diet plans. Looking at sample menus. Checking recipes. It was always there. Hovering in the background. The unwanted soundtrack of my days. I told myself it was necessary. I told myself all kinds of things. I disguised my obsession with food with more acceptable reasons to be thinking about it all the time: I was a "foodie." I enjoyed cooking. This was my art. Learning about nutrition was important. Blah, blah, blah. So much BS. The truth is that I couldn't seem to *not* think about it, so I found ways to explain and justify my preoccupation.

Though the museum we walked around was brand new to me, these kinds of obsessive Thoughts were very familiar. Two decades prior, while I was in Junior High, my mind had been consumed by nearly identical Thoughts, which proved to be the precursor to disordered eating. I dealt with anorexia first, then bulimia, and eventually, bulimarexia—a combination of the two. It started slowly, with just the Thoughts. Then with eating a little less. Then moved on to eating a *lot* less.

By the time I was a high school freshman, the extreme calorie restriction had led to visible, severe weight loss. My worried parents took me to various medical professionals for help. Psychiatrists told me I was depressed and gave me medication, which didn't help. Talking to my overweight, white, male therapist certainly didn't help. He clearly knew *nothing* about being thin. I went to a nutritionist who told me *what* I should eat, but when I looked at her plan that contained multiple servings of fat a day and triple the amount of calories I was currently consuming, I was overcome with panic that I would gain weight. She didn't care about that part—the fear, the panic. She callously told my parents—right in front of me —that either I would choose to eat or I would die, but that she couldn't do anything else for me. All these people told me I had nothing to be afraid of because I wasn't actually fat, but no one taught me how to not be afraid of weight gain. No one addressed the Thoughts. They just told me to stop.

I didn't stop. I didn't feel like I *could* stop. So, I kept losing weight until I was skeletal, desperate, and still no closer to a solution.

When I was a Sophomore, I shared my struggle with a pastor. He told me it was demonic in nature. According to him, all I needed to do was keep my eyes on Jesus, not sin, and pray. I'll admit, that one *did* actually seem to help for a bit. That temporary reprieve offered a ray of hope in the midst of a perpetually dark night. Even that was eventually blotted out when the Thoughts came back, leaving me wondering if I was somehow beyond redemption.

Those first two years of high school were the worst. It was a really dark time for me. I was plagued by embarrassment, guilt, and shame over what I was doing, so I lied to try to hide it, which just heaped more guilt and shame on top. I was drowning in it. I truly didn't want to have an eating disorder. Every bit of what I was doing felt terrible—not to mention affecting my athletic performance—but I couldn't stop because I couldn't make the Thoughts go away. I tried to take the advice of family and friends who cared for me and offered advice, but none of it seemed to really apply. No one understood the inner darkness. At the end of all my efforts, no one had been able to fix me. None of their solutions had helped.

Finally, during my Junior year of High School, I put my foot down with myself and decided it *had* to stop, Thoughts or no Thoughts. No matter how much I want to, I could not allow myself to purge my stomach or starve myself anymore. I felt so bad and was so thin, that I began to believe that being fat, as scary as that was, might be better than continuing on like I was. I fought against my Thoughts, determined to be outwardly normal. I remember my first "normal" meal was a trip to Taco Bell with my Mom, something I hadn't done in ages. It was *brutal*. Sitting there with a full meal in my stomach felt wrong on so many levels.

Despite keeping that meal and many others down, things didn't get better. I felt terrible every day. Every time I ate I had the urge to purge my stomach, but I didn't act on it. *Fat is better than dead.* Every day I made the choice not to outwardly engage in disordered eating. I gained weight back and ended up overweight due to my super slow metabolism. I thought I would die from it. I felt disgusted by myself and my body all the time. No matter what I was doing, the loathing was always with me. Even so, I stuck to my guns as best I could. There were a lot of ups and downs, and I sometimes relapsed, but I kept trying to stop. Every day I shoved the urges down and forced myself to pretend I was past it.

All throughout those years, in the midst of everything going on within me and with my eating, I also had to deal with regular high school. I still went to class, held down a job, remained captain of my sports teams, and dated. I even graduated Valedictorian of my class. By graduation, I felt like I had things locked down. I had will-powered my way through the daily battle long enough that I felt confident I could keep it up. It might feel terrible, but I knew I could keep going and act normally.

I closed that chapter and moved on with my life.

I went to college out of state, leaving behind my hometown and giving myself a fresh start. I was well liked by the other students and made friends quickly. I was respected by the staff for my good behavior, work ethic, and good grades. Things looked acceptable from the outside. I wasn't doing anything outwardly that would cause major alarm to the people around me, but things were far from lovely. I would often binge, alone in my dorm room, and then cry because I wanted to purge so bad. I spent hours exercising to counteract the calories consumed, but as an athlete, no one questioned my time on the treadmill. I was overweight and didn't love my body, but honestly, that was pretty status quo among the rest of the girls on campus, so again, no red flags. Everyday I managed to eat food and keep it in my body. I was not doing anything that would, in my mind, classify as an eating disorder, but I never thought of myself as cured. The way I saw it, I just wasn't "practicing" anymore; in the way that someone might be a Catholic but not a practicing Catholic. I believed I would always have the Thoughts that led to disordered eating, but I also believed I could keep myself from acting on them through willpower.

While at college, I met my husband, who chose me despite the fact that I was still overweight. He was attracted to me and thought I was cute, which was confusing but welcome. The Thoughts were still there all throughout our dating and engagement, but slowly quieting as he showed no signs of bailing. After the first year of marriage, they quieted even more. I found myself bingeing less and I even lost a little weight without trying. His love and acceptance of me and my body were a balm.

During my first pregnancy a few years later the Thoughts got even quieter. I still didn't love my body. I carried very high when I was pregnant and gained more weight than was strictly necessary, but feeling fat while pregnant seemed pretty normal, and feeling fat in a normal way was nice.

Then, after Zoe was born I had the craziest thing happen. I lost all of my pregnancy weight super rapidly and kept losing more. My body was rapidly burning calories because I had a condition that caused my body to produce *way* too much breastmilk. *(TMI? No, that's why you're here.)* I ate all the time, consuming over 3000 calories a day to try to keep up with the physical demands of making that much milk, yet I remained thin. *(It was an extreme overproduction.)* Suddenly, weight management was effortless. I could eat whatever I wanted, and eat a lot of it, and not gain weight. And boy did I eat. Whatever I wanted. Whenever I wanted it. I actually had trouble keeping enough weight on, which was so backward. My weight struggle had been a constant companion for such a long time that I had to relearn how to live and think without it. For the first time since Junior High, the Thoughts were completely silent.

Even after I stopped breastfeeding, chasing a toddler kept me in shape. My weight remained low and the Thoughts stayed away. I continued to eat and think about food in what I considered a normal way. I ate when I was hungry. I ate what I wanted. I didn't feel the need to starve myself. I didn't feel the urge to void my stomach even if I had a bigger meal. I maintained my lower weight easily. I thought about food and my body less than I ever had before and really loved that season of my life.

Then I got pregnant again, had Nadia, walked through those 5 years of hell with my health condition, and the Thoughts were *still* silent. I sometimes shared with others that I *used* to struggle with eating disorders, but, honestly, I forgot about it most of the time. When I did share, I had trouble even connecting with that part of my history. I felt so far removed from it. I hadn't heard the Thoughts in so long that I was forgetting what they sounded like. I genuinely believed I had, somehow, finally overcome that part of my past.

I was wrong.

Here I was, walking around the Getty with my amazing family, in my no-longer-wheelchair-bound body, realizing that the Thoughts were back. Turns out, they had always been there, lying in wait. Dormant. This realization was wildly disappointing and I did not want to accept it. Knowing that these Thoughts were the precursor to outwardly disordered eating was terrifying.

They say, "What doesn't kill you makes you stronger," but I didn't feel stronger; I just felt tired. I had barely caught my breath after the worst of my health issues and was facing a lifetime of managing a chronic condition, which was turning out to be a full-time job. I honestly did not have time for an eating disorder on top of it. Plus, I now had two children to homeschool and care for. Nope. No room in the schedule for this. Yet here it was, an unwanted addition to my to-do list.

Funny enough, it was my recovery, the thing we were most thankful for, that had triggered the return of the Thoughts. I had to be on a liquid diet for several years due to my stomach becoming paralyzed—something we now know was a side-effect of one of my medications. I couldn't get enough calories that way and I dropped a lot of weight from my already thin body. I lost both fat and healthy muscle mass. At one point, I got so thin that my doctor was advocating for a feeding tube. At 5'5", I had gotten down to 111 pounds and 11% body fat. I was wearing a size 0/1 pant and looked incredibly unhealthy. My hair was dull, my face was pale, and my skin was dry. I had no muscle at all. The little bit of tissue I had was hanging off my bones due to the extreme atrophy of being bed bound. Even so, most of my female friends were super jealous because I was skinny. They saw it as a positive, something I found tremendously confusing.

Eventually, I got off that medication and slowly gained back most of my stomach function. Once I started eating more, I also started to gain back some of the lost weight. Technically, that was good news. In fact, it was what I had been working hard to achieve. To get better. To get stronger. To eat normally. It was exactly what needed to happen for my body to be healthy. Yet, somehow, the much needed weight gain triggered all the old Thoughts. It was as if my brain could not distinguish between healthy weight gain and unhealthy weight gain. It saw all weight gain as bad.

Logically, I knew I needed to keep gaining weight. I still didn't have enough body fat to maintain healthy hormone function, but I could pinch some fat on my stomach, which was where I always gained first, and my mind was freaking out. *Thoughts. Thoughts. Thoughts.* I kept telling myself it was a good thing. I'd been telling myself that for months, ever since I started noticing the panic around meal times. Or when I stepped on the scale. Or when my clothing felt tight. Or when I had to buy bigger sizes. I *told* myself it was good, but it didn't *feel* good, regardless of the logic. All the logic in the world wasn't helping. I *knew* it was illogical. I had always known that. I knew on some level that my issues with my body and food had always been in my head. During my eating disorder days I was very thin and felt compelled to keep losing weight anyway. I knew that it wasn't about the weight, I just didn't really know what it *was* about.

Just days before our trip to the museum, all of this reached a tipping point. I was in the bedroom changing with the door closed when Chris came in to get something. I immediately turned my body and hid my exposed chest and stomach from him. I finished dressing, then turned to find him in the same spot, just staring at me. I still remember the look on his face so clearly: surprise, hurt, concern. I had shared with him about my past, so he knew—at least on some level—what this meant.

"When did this happen?" he asked, with a pained look on his face. "When did you start hiding from me?"

I answered as truthfully as I could and said, "I don't know."

I really didn't. I did know the volume had been rising for a while. Slowly at first, but it was now dangerously loud. I couldn't pinpoint the moment things went from run-of-the-mill body image issues to these Thoughts, but they were here now. I had hoped to get things quietly under control without alerting anyone to the issue. I didn't need anyone's judgement, concern, or pity. My shame was plenty.

I was losing control and now Chris knew it too, which made it so much more real. Over Christmas break (before the museum) I had mindlessly plowed through a bunch of holiday sweets, then panicked about the impending weight gain. I had no way to void my stomach without my family knowing about it since we were all at home on break, so I lied about not feeling well, saying my stomach felt off. Then I proceeded to head to the bathroom, lock the door, kneel before the toilet and empty my stomach with everyone's full awareness and sympathy that I didn't feel well. I was thankful to have an excuse to lay in bed alone, because I couldn't face my daughters, or look my husband in the eye. In all the years of dealing with my eating disorders, I had never felt as ashamed as I did in that moment.

As awful as that was, I found myself fantasizing about doing it again—to choose whatever I wanted, regardless of whether it was good for me or not, and then eat until I was numb. I hadn't repeated the experience, but only through teeth gritted, white knuckled, willpower. If I'm honest, I probably would have acted on the impulse more, except that our tiny apartment had one bathroom and thin walls, which made concealment nearly impossible. I did not want my daughters to suspect anything.

My daughters. As I watched them explore the museum—talking, laughing, making jokes, being silly, asking genuine questions, learning, being curious, and just generally being their amazing selves, I felt such a jumble of emotions. All the fierce love I felt for them was mixed with the fear of what their futures would be if I didn't get this thing with my body and food figured out. The very idea that they might struggle the way that I had was so overwhelmingly sad that I thought it would crush me.

They deserve better than this. They deserve better than me. I can't do this again! I can't. Not with them in the house. Not where they could become aware. I will not doom them to continue this horrific cycle. I do not want them to have a Mom who deals with this. I'm not in Junior High anymore for God's sake! What is wrong with me? I should be thankful. I should be happy. I should have my act together by now!

I desperately wanted them to have healthy relationships with their bodies. They were lovely and I hoped they always knew it. Yet, how could I possibly teach them something that I did not understand for myself? I had been trying for nearly 20 years to figure this thing out and had failed every time. I had tried everything I could think of; BUT I COULD NOT CRACK THE CODE! What hope did I have this time around? What hope was there for them? It seemed like very little. I was so very tired of this. I was spiraling and could see the dark pit that was disordered eating opening up before me and I was perched dangerously on the edge. Falling in felt like more of a question of *when*, than *if*. I was just delaying the inevitable.

Thank God we went to the museum.

Chapter 2

An Ancient Goddess Intrigues

As I meandered the museum and studiously compared my body with the other women in the building, I suppose it only made sense that I would also compare my body to those depicted in the art. I wasn't consciously aware that I was doing this. I certainly wasn't doing it intentionally, but I know I was because of what happened next.

We were moving through the museum at a pretty quick clip. The kids were still young enough that they weren't prone to standing and pondering any piece for very long, so we mostly just kept pace with them. However, when I found myself in a room of white, marble statues, I slowed down to really appreciate the pieces, trusting my husband to corral the kids and planning to catch up with them in the next section.

I have always been drawn to Greek and Roman sculpture. I find the white marble beautiful and the figures' serene faces make me feel peaceful. Moreover, I am impressed by the level of skill involved in carving such intricate shapes and patterns into stone. I imagine the process to be nerve wracking. In a painting, though still requiring incredible skill, at least you can sometimes remove a mistake or paint over it and not redo the entire canvas. If you chip off a bit of stone that shouldn't be chipped off, you can't reattach it. No do-overs. No mistakes.

I wandered from statue to statue, pondering such things, when I found myself looking into the face of a maiden. She was sitting on a tree stump, right leg crossed over her left knee, and was either putting on or taking off one of her sandals. Like most Greek and Roman carvings, she was totally naked. That meant that I could see her body freely displayed before me. When I stopped to look at her and make my comparisons, I had a thought that was so shocking, so unexpected, that it pulled me right out of the Thoughts that were always running in some part of my mind. The thought I had was, "Her body looks pretty similar to mine."

That stopped me right in my tracks.

I paused to really examine the body before me. She looked like a woman of average size and shape. She had soft curves and was not muscular. Her breasts were of average size (though she clearly she hadn't nursed any babies as they were in the correct hemisphere, unlike mine). Her thighs were full. If she stood up, there would be no gap. Her arms lacked definition. Her stomach was not hanging over or protruding, but it wasn't washboard flat either. It looked soft and rounded, with love handles and some fat visible in the area just below her belly button...right where mine was a little soft too. There was a clear crease just above her belly button where her natural waist would be. You could tell that if she bent over any farther there would be small fat rolls.

Then, I looked at the label and was shocked to find that I was examining a depiction of the Goddess of Beauty. One of my first thoughts was that I wished I could see her jeans size. Okay, I realize she wouldn't have actually worn denim, but I wanted to see, because I was pretty sure she would be wearing bigger pants than I had on. Maybe a bigger shirt size as well. Regardless of her exact size, I had been every size from a 0 to a 14 over the last 15 years. Meaning, at some point in my life, I was *that* size regardless of what the number was. And possibly her shape as well, based on the similarities I was seeing. This meant, at some time in my life, maybe multiple times, my body could have been very similar to that of the Goddess of Beauty. She and I could have shared jeans. As I stood there and scrutinized every inch of her body, comparing it to mine piece by piece, I felt an overwhelming sense of confusion. How was this possible? How could we have similar bodies if she was the ancient standard of feminine beauty? I had *never* felt beautiful.

Clearly, my body size and shape wasn't the real issue here, and that was not exactly news to me. Conceptually, I had learned that the standards of feminine beauty were cultural and shifted with time. In America today, looking tan is considered attractive. In the past, that was a negative thing because it meant you had to work in the sun, a sign of low social standing. Historically, thinness was a sign of poverty and wasn't a desirable trait. Even as recently as the 1950s, the main advertisement for women was how to *gain* weight if you were too skinny, which was considered unattractive. I *knew* this. I also knew that what I saw in magazines was often highly edited, meaning that even the models didn't really look like the models. The truth was, I knew a *lot* of facts and information that *should* have made me okay with my perfectly normal body, but they didn't. They never had.

Knowing that the ideal body size was subject to cultural standards hadn't kept me from hating mine. As I stood comparing this goddess' body to mine, I knew that hating my body had nothing to do with its size, because I had hated it at *every* stage of weight gain and loss.

When I was deep into anorexic seasons, I was scarily thin, and I hated my body.

When I was a healthy weight: I hated it.

Overweight: hated it.

All the facts and information about ever changing beauty ideals had done absolutely nothing for me. If anything, it just made me feel crazy. Because, despite *knowing* my thoughts weren't rational, I couldn't seem to change them. None of the information I collected moved me any closer to a solution for myself.

I wish I could say how many books I read on the subject of weight loss. How much time I spent on the internet scouring blogs. I wish I knew how many hours I spent trying to change my body into something I found acceptable. I'm curious to know those numbers in light of the fact that the path to my salvation came to me in an instant without any effort or forethought on my part. It was just an innocent question, just a few words that flitted through my brain of their own accord as I stood staring at this statue:

I wonder what it would have been like...

to be...

her.

That was it. Nothing profound. But it was the spark that started everything.

I had heard women talk about self-love. I had read about the importance of a positive body image. Both made sense conceptually, but I had no personal experience or context for either. They didn't compute for me on any level. Every single woman I knew wished her body was different. In fact, most of them were actively working to change their bodies. The ones who weren't *still* didn't like how they looked. They had simply given up—but definitely weren't happy about it. My goals weren't that lofty. I was aiming for tolerance...or at least a cessation of harmful actions like bingeing and purging. To love my body? *HA!* Mythical. A fairy tale. Well, in this case, I suppose it literally was. Here was a woman who would have *actually* loved her body, but she wasn't real!

As I stood there, I realized that the Goddess of Beauty was perhaps not quite as mythical as I first thought. I do not believe Greek or Roman gods or goddesses were real beings, but I wondered if there had been a real-life woman who served as the model for this statue. That would make perfect sense. If that was the case, then in some way, she *was* real. There was some woman who existed at one point in time whose body was considered worthy to represent the Goddess. Her body had been deemed the epitome of beauty, then engraved in stone to stand as a marker for thousands of years as a representation of the Goddess. I thought of that real life woman who had modeled for this sculpture. I imagined that *she* would not have desired to change her body. It was objectively perfect in her time. (I mean, the artist chose *that* body for a reason.) This was something I could only fathom being true for *that* woman. It seemed a singular occurrence in all of history.

I knew I had to continue with the tour. I had been standing there for a while and my husband and kids had long since moved on, so I hurried to catch up, but I was now on the hunt for more likenesses of the Goddess of Beauty, both the Greek Aphrodite and her Roman counterpart, Venus. There were a number of other depictions throughout the museum. In the same room as the original statue was a bronze Venus, with a slightly fuller figure. There were also a number of paintings depicting Venus and Mars, including one where, according to my understanding of BMI, the depicted Venus would be decidedly overweight. I took in each new image, both confused and intrigued by all that I was seeing.

Curious, I pulled out my phone and did a quick Google for statues of Aphrodite. I saw a number of images similar to what I was seeing at the Getty. Some, like Venus de Milo, I had seen before, but I had never really *looked* at like I was looking now. I had never really *seen* how they were shaped. I was particularly impacted by a depiction of Aphrodite crouching, which clearly showed rolling waves of fat on her belly. I thought, *Yep, that's pretty much what mine looks like when I bend like that too!* I think it is how the bellies of most women look when they crouch down, yet I had always been embarrassed by it. Her rolls were not edited out, but clearly displayed. The model for this statue wouldn't have been chosen *in spite* of her rolls, but perhaps *because* of them. Fascinating.

I tried to see the rest of the art all around me, not wanting to miss anything, but I couldn't focus. I was distracted, pondering all of these images. *Multiple depictions meant multiple models. Perhaps not as unique as I first thought.* Mulling this over, the mythical goddesses, and all the possible real life women who modeled for the statues, fused into one being in my mind.

I thought of this being simply as…Aphrodite.

She became more than any one depiction or one person alone. She transcended the cultural and historical parameters for beauty. For me, Aphrodite represented a woman who truly loved her body, just like it was, with no need or desire to change it. She represented a woman who truly loved herself.

I found myself completely absorbed in wondering what life would have been like for such a woman. What would it have been like to wake up each day and know that your body was the standard for beauty? What would it have been like to not have any need or desire to change it? What would it have been like to be Aphrodite? To *really* love your body, exactly like it was?

I drew a blank.

I had nothing to pull from. No real life examples. No personal experience.

As I considered this woman—*who truly loved herself*—something in my soul, something that had been buried for a lot of years, stirred.

I think…

I think it was hope.

These questions took my mind captive. To say I was intrigued by her was an understatement. I was enthralled. I continued to ponder Aphrodite with each footfall in the museum, too busy thinking of her to bother comparing myself to other women. As I sat on a wire chair in the inner courtyard of the Getty, eating the lunch I had been so obsessed with mere moments before, I found myself so distracted by my thoughts of her that I barely cared about the food once the edge was off my hunger. Back at home, while my hands were occupied chopping veggies for dinner, I let my mind wander to thoughts of Aphrodite. I pondered her as I lay my head on my pillow that night. As the light poured through my window the next morning, I woke with her on my heart...and a plan taking shape in my mind.

Chapter 3

A Hope of a Different Life

Life is life, and I had to get back to my normal routine, responsibilities, and duties; but, whenever I was doing tasks that didn't require my full focus, my mind was on Aphrodite. I spent time just pondering what life would have been like for her, mulling it over in the back of my mind all throughout my day. I didn't have any agenda at this point. I was just immensely intrigued by what life would be like for a woman who truly loved her body exactly as it was, a woman who could go through life without any thought of needing to change herself in any way. It was fascinating to me because it was so unfamiliar. She was an oddity and I found myself studying her like a scientist would study a newly discovered animal or plant species. Plus, uncovering her secrets was a deeply engrossing thought experiment, that, frankly, was quite a bit more fun than what was normally in my mind.

As I began my daily chores, smoothing the cotton sheets of our bed, I imagined she didn't have any need to compare her body with the body of others.

While wet to the elbows with dishwater, I pondered a woman who cared for her body because it was her greatest asset, not a flawed vessel needing to be changed.

Wiping down the counters with the smell of lemon in my nose, I considered a woman for whom conversations of diets and exercise plans would not have applied, which meant she could have talked of other things. Pursued other things. Dreamed of things that were significantly more important than a number on the scale.

As I dumped the warm laundry on the bed and began to fold, I imagined a woman who looked in the mirror and felt no shame upon seeing her reflection. A woman who got dressed and felt completely content. Happy even.

As my kids and I took our morning walk and breathed in the brisk air, I imagined the mind of Aphrodite. I thought it must be a mind free of all the mental garbage that clogged up mine. I imagined how calm and spacious that mind must be.

Sliding the homeschool books into their places at the end of the school day, I wondered, *how far could a woman go in life if she loved her body and never wasted any time or energy with negative thoughts about herself?* I imagined pretty far.

In truth, a woman with the perfect body, who completely loved that body, could still have had other character flaws or others aspects of herself that she took issue with. It just seemed unlikely to me. First of all, based on my own experience, I was pretty sure that if you didn't have issues with your body, then everything else was minor. Secondly, her body was part of her. A lot of my personal focus was on my body, but the Aphrodite in my mind was confident about all aspects of herself. She loved all of herself, body included. So, while the concepts of body image and self-love might actually be separate, they were both part of the Aphrodite I was imagining and melded seamlessly into this woman I was inventing in my mind.

With her on my mind all throughout my day, I became more aware of myself. I paid more attention to what I was doing and wondered, *Would Aphrodite have done this?* While I performed daily tasks, half of my mind imagined what she would be thinking and feeling if she was doing the same task. A woman who loves herself and her body—*what would she think about?* The other half of my mind was examining what I was thinking and feeling; and the juxtaposition was shocking. I hadn't realized how bad things truly were inside of me until I compared my mind to hers.

My thoughts about my body were extremely negative, but I was also brutal on myself as a person. I beat myself up in my own mind. I chastised myself for the smallest failures. I called myself names, things I would never in a million years say to another person; things that would be considered verbal abuse if they were said to me by someone else. I could even find flaws with my successes. Nothing was ever good enough. Ultimately, I believed that *I* was not good enough. I picked apart every word or phrase from others, trying to see if they thought I wasn't good enough too.

I remember one particular day, I was in the middle of homeschooling my kids and I started thinking about Aphrodite and what she would do if she were in my shoes and homeschooling my kids. I imagined her being calm, confident, peaceful, and loving. I imagined her extending love to her children from the overflowing well of love she had inside herself.

Then, I tuned into my own thinking. The thoughts were racing and spiraling, so I got out my laptop, opened a blank word document, and let what I was thinking come out onto the page. I didn't censor it, I just let it flow. When it was all out, I went back to homeschool. All throughout the morning, I would just walk by and write down whatever I was thinking about myself.

That afternoon after homeschool was over I went back and looked at all that I had written down. I was shocked. There were all the normal thoughts about my body and food, but I also wrote things like: *I'm a terrible mother. I'm the worst mom in the world. I'm so sad my kids have me as a mom. I'm completely failing these kids. I'm such a screw up. What's wrong with me? I need to be more patient. I need to be more loving. I need to be better. I need to be more than I am. We never laugh. I'm no fun. My kids are going to end up in therapy. They would be better off without me.*

As my eyes took it all in, I thought, *No wonder I feel like crap all the time.* It was awful. Viewing it in black and white, I could see that some of it clearly wasn't true. There was no way I was the *worst* mother in the world. I had never beaten my children, starved them, locked them in a closet, or tried to murder them, so I could make a strong case against that one. A lot of it really *felt* true though, and I got a good look at how much self-loathing I had for myself. I was about as far as I could imagine from a woman who loved herself, very un-Aphrodite-ish to say the least.

To be fair, I didn't hate *everything* about myself, but I did feel a deep longing to simply be someone different. It was like I wanted to escape from myself. Not my *life*—I loved my family and my friends. I was regularly in awe that someone like my husband chose me. I was flabbergasted by the amazing women who wanted to know my opinion or just spend time with me. *I* just didn't like spending time with me. I wasn't sure when or how I got to that place, but it had been that way for as long as I could remember. Sure, I had done some things I was proud of, but they were more about my achievements than anything to do with me as a person. If I took away all the things I had done and only Lorrie (the person) remained, the remnant would have been less than worthless in my mind. Ergo, I was always pushing, always striving, always trying to be better. To be different. To be more.

As I continued to catch glimpses of the mind and life of Aphrodite throughout my day, I saw the reality of my life come into focus. Love for myself was non-existent. I was paying attention to my inner world for the first time and realized how deeply unhappy I was. And I didn't want to keep going like I was.

I don't want this life anymore! I don't like it! I want something different. I want to stop feeling awful all the time. I want more. I want to be happy like her. I want to think of other things like she would rather than obsessing about my body and exercise and how many calories I'm eating. I want to really live. I want her *life.*

And that sparked a delicious idea.

Chapter 4

One Question to Change it All

The fact was, I did not love my body. I hated it—or at least something very close to hate. I honestly did not see a way to change that. The way I saw it, my body had been failing me in one way or another my whole life.

My body was the reason I couldn't go as far as I wanted in my sports career: too short.

My body was the reason I spent 5 years of my life in a wheelchair: defective.

My body was never the right size: always too fat or the wrong shape to look nice in clothes.

It wasn't just me who thought that. My family had regularly commented on *my body* and how odd it was—they told me I was built like a boy, that my thighs looked like I was a bodybuilder, that my boobs were too small, and my butt was too big. They were mostly teasing, but I knew there was truth in there too. When I was a Senior in High School I remember standing with two of my friends and someone commenting on our body types. They labeled one as a classic pear shape, one as a classic hourglass figure, "And, Lorrie, you're kind of shaped like a french fry." I'm not sure if they meant a straight cut or a crinkle cut, but it wasn't positive either way.

These observations about my body just *were*, and I didn't see any hope of my thoughts on the matter ever changing. Feelings aside, I knew things needed to change in my behavior. I needed to find a way to stop harming my body, even if only for Zoe and Nadia, and not myself. As much as I wanted to turn things around for the sake of my daughters, I also knew *I* was the last person to be consulted on such matters owing to how horribly I had botched it thus far.

As I thought about Aphrodite and imagined her life, I knew for sure that her life lacked the things that were most destructive in mine—like the emotional binge eating, disordered eating, and self-directed verbal abuse. I thought: *Maybe I could just fake it. Maybe I don't really need to love myself. Maybe I can just imagine what Aphrodite would have done and do that.* I could continue to imagine a woman who actually loved herself living my life, just the way I had been doing for the last several days. I could figure out what she would do in each situation and then do *that* instead of whatever I had been doing that clearly was not working.

Maybe it doesn't have to be real to work. Maybe I don't have to really love myself. Maybe I can just imitate loving myself. My internal compass is broken, but Aphrodite can be my guide.

I felt so much hope at the idea.

This could actually work. I felt like I had been thrown a buoy just when I was in danger of drowning. After nearly giving up hope for good, I had stumbled across one last course of action to try. A Hail Mary in the last seconds of a losing game. The plan I created was not elegant or complicated. It was simple, and inspired by something I hadn't thought of in years.

I grew up in the Midwest, in the Bible Belt, during the "What Would Jesus Do?" craze. I remember stringing beads with the letters WWJD onto thin leather strips to wear as bracelets.

Anytime we saw it, we were supposed to ask ourselves, "What Would Jesus Do?" and then do that.

Well, why wouldn't the same thing work here? True, it was a mythical goddess rather than the son of God, but the principle seemed to still work. So, I switched out "Jesus" with "Aphrodite," which seems completely sacrilegious when said that way, but was not meant to be. In any and every situation I would simply ask myself the question, *What Would Aphrodite Do?* i.e., what would a woman who loved herself and her body do in this situation? What would *I* do if I loved myself and my body? Then I would do that. WWAD. I would just do whatever she would have done. I would act *as if* I loved myself based on how I imagined she would act. I would try to think what she would think. I would say what she would say.

Okay, okay, of course I wouldn't *truly* love myself with this plan—*don't be ridiculous*—but perhaps it would keep me from the Thoughts. Keep me from disordered eating. Even if it was fake, maybe it would let me present a decent example to my daughters. It certainly couldn't be any worse than the way things currently were.

Yes. I could do this. I could act in loving ways even if I would never really love myself, even if I wasn't really lovable. The whole charade would definitely be worth it.

WWAD.

Game. On.

Part 2: Learning from Aphrodite

Chapter 5

Where Would Aphrodite Start?

Day 1 of the WWAD method.

I was barely upright before the kids were asking for breakfast. With the mention of breakfast came the Thought onslaught. I decided the first place to apply my new WWAD method was to meals, as they were producing the greatest amount of stress in my life. My daughters had this odd notion that they needed to be fed every few hours, so I had the privilege of entertaining negative thoughts about food and its effect on my body multiple times throughout the day. *Yay!* (Read: sarcasm. Complete and total sarcasm.)

In truth, I can't blame it all on the kids, because it started long before they were born. Thoughts about what to eat, when to eat it, and how much to consume had taken up an inordinate amount of time and mental energy over the course of my life. I had spent countless hours researching diet plans, learning about weight loss methods, and planning meals that fit various guidelines in an effort to figure out how to eat correctly so I wouldn't be fat. Basically, I went back and forth between two extremes in terms of food during my life. One extreme was to hyper-control everything about my meals. The other was to control nothing and make everything allowed.

When I was in hyper-control-mode, I would decide on a set of guidelines to govern my eating, and then follow them religiously. These plans centered on calories consumed, macronutrient ratios, and/or the types of foods that were allowed. The plans were based on the teachings of various people that I had come across in books, articles, documentaries, blogs, etc. I would take their ideas and create detailed charts involving food and exercise with everything precisely mapped out and printed. Then I would follow it to the letter. Sometimes, I would construct my own method, but this was always a compilation of other people's teachings and the main focus was always weight loss, even if I convinced myself and other people it was for other, more noble reasons— like overall better health.

I was extremely rigid in executing these plans. If I was tracking calories, I didn't eat anything I couldn't accurately track, and if I didn't know the exact ingredients for a food or its exact amount, I would not eat it. There were many times when I skipped the opportunity to eat a fun treat at an event or enjoy a meal out in order to be able to weigh, measure, and control my food at home. I knew I could not trust myself to eat even a single bite off plan or I would likely eat everything in the house and spiral out of control for days or weeks or months. So, I worked hard to keep myself firmly under control.

I felt severely restricted, but I also felt safe when I lived life this way. The ultra-rigid diets eliminated my own thoughts and desires from the equation. I simply disregarded all the signals from my body and followed the plan. I'd proven that I could not trust my body or myself when it came to food, so it made sense to follow someone else's formula. They would tell me what to do and I would do it. Then, if I gained weight, it would not be my fault, but the fault of the plan.

Confession: while I did not outright "cheat" on these plans—because I wouldn't have been able to handle the guilt—I did find ways to stretch the rules. I would lick spoons—sometimes I would even "accidentally" get them dirty again so that I *had* to lick them again. *Oops! Dropped it...again.* I would leave excess in the blender or bowl to "clean out." I would move food from one container to another unnecessarily, then eat any crumbs left behind. (Waste not, want not, right?) I would "even up" slices of cake or dessert—for aesthetics. I often baked dessert "for the family," even if I didn't have any, just so I could lick the blender paddles. I generally tried to eat the most possible food without being "off" the diet plan. I had elaborate guidelines for what "counted." A spilled raisin—or five or ten—didn't count as long as they weren't in a bowl. Scraps off my kids' plates didn't count if it was too little to save for tomorrow. I spent a lot of time rationalizing ways to consume these phantom calories that were neither here nor there.

Back in college, during one of these hyper-control-mode phases, I read a diet book that said you should never eat a portion that was larger than the size of your fist—because that was the size of the human stomach when it wasn't stretched out. It totally made sense in theory, and I was fully committed to the method, believing this was the answer to all my woes. I followed it to the letter and felt proud of myself for eating "right." The only problem was that I was always hungry. Always. I kept waiting for my stomach to shrink like the book said it would, but that didn't appear to be happening. I ended up eating more food overall than I would have if I had just eaten a regular meal, albeit in fist-sized portions.

I found myself trying to find ways to follow the diet, but also eat more food at each sitting. A fist sized portion of lettuce was next to nothing, so surely that couldn't be a whole meal. Maybe the authors meant a fist sized portion once it was chewed? Which was *way* more. I ended up building a version of this diet around how to eat foods that looked really big on my plate and required lots of chewing but that would still only be the size of my fist once they landed in my stomach. For the year I was on this diet I could often be seen taking normal food and pounding and compacting it into a smaller portion to see if it "fit." It was ridiculous. I did not lose any weight on this diet. Though I did gain some mealtime-guilt after the first couple of weeks—anytime I ate a portion size larger than my fist. This particular diet fed my food obsession more than any of the other plans because I was eating all the time, which meant I was always thinking about food.

While I did feel safer in hyper-control-mode, I was also tense all the time. I missed out on a lot of simple pleasures to stick to the diets. I remember sitting with my husband and daughters one Sunday morning, watching them down piles of pancakes —that I made!—drenched in syrup and feeling so much resentment towards them for their ability to eat freely without having to count calories. *This isn't fair! I hate this! Why am I always the one who has to miss out?* As much as I disliked the deprivation, sitting there being miserable still seemed *way* better than needing to buy bigger pants. The very thought of that produced huge doses of panic—avoid at all cost! It wasn't fun, but, at least in this mode I could be proud of myself for my ability to do something "right," i.e. follow the diet. I mentally gave myself gold stars for not cheating and extra gold stars if I felt awful during the process.

Gold stars or not, monitoring everything I ate was extremely time consuming and, frankly, not sustainable if I wanted to do anything else with my life (which is part of why I had never been able to maintain the hyper-control-mode indefinitely). The only real alternative I could figure out to this rigidity was to swing really far in the other direction and make everything allowed. The old "all things in moderation" adage never worked for me. These were off-limits, fattening foods and if they were now fair game, good luck getting me to stop before I had consumed my fill—and then some. The idea of having a little and then forcing myself to stop was a worse torture than having none at all. Either I had them never or I had them always. That was the only it that worked for me.

While in everything-allowed-mode, instead of sorting food into good or bad, healthy or unhealthy, fattening or slimming; it was all just food. I could eat what I wanted, when I wanted it, and however much of it I wanted. The handful of times in my life that I did this, I gained weight. Sometimes I gained a lot of weight—like my freshman year of college. People joke about gaining The Freshman 15, but I gained The Freshman 30, which was mostly due to the food, but also partially due to suddenly having a college desk job rather than high school sports practice.

The very first time I went into everything-allowed-mode was actually my Junior year of high school when I was trying to stop acting out on my disordered eating. My solution was to *just eat* and not think about it so much. The results were nothing short of disastrous. As soon as everything was allowed, I ate every off-limits, low-quality, sugary thing in sight. Somehow, the more I consumed, the more I wanted. It was like my body was making up for all the missed food over the last few years, hoarding it in case there was another self-imposed famine. The result was not only weight gain—along with the need to buy new clothes, which was its own special kind of hell—but an even deeper sense of self-loathing, more evidence that my body was the enemy, and proof that my hunger and desire for food could not be trusted.

With each pendulum swing I would have the same results: on one end, exhaustion from the rigidity, but with weight loss; on the other end, more enjoyment of daily life, but with weight gain from overeating. Neither worked long term and I knew I needed an alternative to the back-and-forth. Something that would prevent excess body fat accumulation, but also let me reclaim some sanity! I knew I absolutely needed an outside reference point, but I could not go on another strict diet.

My WWAD method seemed to meet the criteria. Aphrodite would be my reference point as I tackled meal times, so the pressure was off of me to know what to do. There was also no diet plan, because I knew that Aphrodite would not have been on a diet. Diets are what we do to lose weight and change our body. Aphrodite would never have needed to do that, because her body was already amazing.

She would show me how a woman who loved her body (just as it was) would eat.

I was very eager to put my new WWAD methodology into practice. I longed to be free of all of the Thoughts and all of the associated pain, and I really wanted this to work. All I had to do was discover what Aphrodite would eat. She could tell me when to eat and how much. Then, I would do that. I only had to do what she would have done.

Okay, so...what *would* Aphrodite eat?

As I sat and pondered the question, rather than getting answers, I came up with more questions: *Were there foods she wouldn't eat? Was it all allowed? Was it really "all things in moderation?" Would she have rules about food at all? Would she eat desserts? When would she eat? How often would she eat? How much would she eat? (Dear God, please let it be more than a fist-sized portion!)* I would ponder all of these questions in my mind whenever I was going throughout my day, hoping some answers would come.

They didn't.

It took a little time to work it out, but I realized I was still in my own head too much. I was filtering the questions through my personal history and dieting paradigm. The truth was that Aphrodite would have approached mealtimes from a fundamentally different place than me. I was bringing all of my emotional baggage to the table. She didn't have any of that. Aphrodite would never have been on a "diet" in the conventional sense of the word. I wasn't even sure how to approach these questions apart from the idea of diets, meal plans, and calorie counting. The only thing I could think of was to try to put myself in her headspace and just imagine the whole process from start to finish.

The next day, when the kids were finished with homeschool, fed, and intent on playing in their playroom for a while, I snuck away for a session with Aphrodite. I sat on my couch and pulled my legs up, wrapping my arms around them, and sat quietly with my eyes closed. I tried to insert myself into Aphrodite's mind, to imagine what it would be like to be her, a woman whose body was the standard of beauty. A woman who genuinely loved her body and didn't have any need or desire to change it. I tried to imagine what that would feel like. I tried to imagine what her thoughts would be like: *I love this body just the way it is. I'm so thankful that this is my body.*

Then, I tried to imagine her eating a meal, hoping to figure out what was on her plate, but I couldn't get there. It was so completely out of context. I couldn't just jump from "I love myself" to mid-meal. There is always some point when we are not eating. *Then* comes the decision to eat. *Then* the getting of food. *Then* the actual eating. So, I would have to start at some point before the meal. I thought about starting at the decision to eat, but I realized that wasn't far enough back either.

Her entire perspective would be different from mine. She *already* loved herself. Just like she was. That love would have colored every aspect of the process leading up to a meal, including life before the process even started. If I was going to do this, I would need to look at all of those areas. Ugh. This would take time. Maybe a lot. Well, in for a penny, in for a pound I suppose. It couldn't be more exhausting than the way things already were.

All right, Aphrodite, let's start at the beginning...or, perhaps more accurately, a little before the beginning.

Chapter 6

What Would Aphrodite Do When She Wasn't Eating?

I opened my eyes and thought for a minute. When I wasn't eating, my mind could often be found obsessing about food. What would it be like for someone who had never had disordered eating, who did not have any baggage or trauma around food, diets, or mealtimes? For someone who wasn't interested in losing weight? Would she be thinking like me? *No. Definitely not.* I concluded that she wouldn't be thinking about food all the time. Why would she? Most of my thoughts —outside of actual meals—were about my longing for forbidden food, beating myself up about past meals, and researching weight loss. If I took those parts away, there wasn't a lot left–just the basic thoughts of planning meals, buying food, and preparing it. Those things would come without the drama that surrounded those times for me. Man, it would be so nice to only think about food when I was shopping for it or cooking it.

I adjusted my legs to a more comfortable position, closed my eyes again, breathed deep, and turned on my imagination. Up until now, I had really only considered Aphrodite's thoughts, but I needed a more concrete vision of her for the work I was about to do, so I constructed an Aphrodite avatar in my mind. I took the statue I had seen at the Getty and adjusted it a bit.

First, she needed some clothes. Even though my concept of Aphrodite could work in any time period, I couldn't quite see her in modern clothes, so I gave her a blue, loose-fitting toga with a decorative belt. The statue I saw had her hair up, but in my vision her hair was a golden-brown and worn down in loose waves—what I imagined it would look like if she took her hair down from the updo she had worn in the sculpture.

Then, I tried to imagine her living her life. I tried to picture her doing something that was not related to mealtimes so that her thoughts wouldn't be on that at all. I let various images float through my mind. I imagined her taking a walk, shopping in the market, reading a book, and tidying the house. Everyday things.

I chose to zero in on her walking around a market, looking at the wares in the various stalls. Then I asked, *If she was doing something mundane like this, what would she be thinking? What would she be feeling? What would someone like her think about all day? Someone who loved herself just like she was? Someone who had no need to think about weight loss?* Then, in my mind, I watched her closely.

Her head was up, shoulders comfortably back, chest open. There was a slight smile on her lips. She looked happy. She looked like she was enjoying herself. She walked from stall to stall, carrying a woven brown basket. She took a moment to pick up a bar of hand-made soap and smell it. She met the stall owner's eye when he spoke to her and laughed easily about something he said. Her eyes were clear and untroubled. She was so...*present*. Yes! That's the word. Present. Like the only thing she was thinking about was what was right in front of her.

Lesson 1: Aphrodite is present for her life.

Wow. I released the vision of Aphrodite and opened my eyes. I had my first answer and it felt like I had just won a million dollars.

I sat there, on the couch in my living room, and examined my life. I thought about my days. I thought about the amount of time I felt bad and how much of that was related directly or indirectly to food and my body. In that moment I realized I could feel a lot better even if I never fixed my relationship with food. If I were to simply stop feeling awful about food outside of meal times, my life would improve so much! If I thought of *other things* anytime I wasn't eating, I would get 90% of my thought life back.

I stopped the vision and opened my eyes. I wanted to apply this before taking in any more lessons from Aphrodite. *What Would Aphrodite Do? If she were me and had my exact life, how would she be present in it? What would she be doing right now? What would she think about right now? What would I do if I simply wasn't thinking negatively about myself, my diet, my weight, my body, or upcoming meals?*

I thought she would enjoy *this* moment. If she loved herself as she was, right now, and there was no pull to change or be different, then any moment would be as good as the next. I was always waiting and anticipating a future where I weighed less and liked myself more. I was convinced that when I was thin, I would be happy. That is why I was so urgent to get there. Aphrodite was not waiting for her happiness. She loved herself today. She loved her body today. There was no future moment when she would love herself more than right now. The love she felt for herself would have been a constant presence, filling each moment of her days, following her wherever she went.

If my every moment was filled with love, I might want to be present for it too! Usually, I was checking out of my present moment because it sucked. I kept busy to keep from being alone with myself because all my thoughts felt terrible. Quiet and stillness were to be avoided at all costs. Maybe someday I could sit alone with myself…when I had a better body and my life was in order. Not Aphrodite. She wouldn't be striving for some future moment that would be better. Right now would be as equally amazing as next week, and she would have been right there for both.

I looked around me, I mean *really* looked for the first time in a while. I tried to actually *see* it. We had recently moved and this place was *so* much bigger and nicer than the tiny apartment we had previously occupied. It was an older home with a ton of detail and history. I fully focused on what was around me. I took a minute to appreciate all the original, wood framed windows and natural light we got no matter the hour. I took in the simple wonder and beauty of a golden sunbeam shining on the wooden floor. I noticed our built in bookcases and arched doorways, which made me so happy when we first moved in but that I hadn't thought about in weeks. I looked up at the vaulted ceiling, which had wooden beams with designs hand painted on them and appreciated the uniqueness of our space. I felt an overwhelming sense of gratitude for our current home.

More than the gratitude or anything else, in that moment I mostly felt…okay. I realized I felt okay for the first time in a while simply by letting in some other thoughts, some beauty, some stillness. Nothing profound, no major revelations, no overwhelming feelings of awesome, I just wasn't thinking the Thoughts that felt so bad. It felt so nice to not feel bad. I felt lighter. It was such a relief to just be in a moment without feeling the constant, gnawing urgency to change my body. I hadn't realized how heavy that weight was or how tiring it was to always be carrying it around.

So...*What Would Aphrodite Do now?* Well, houses are nice, but people are better. I got up and went to see my two daughters. I went into their playroom and asked them what they were playing. Then, I gave them my *full* attention for a few minutes. They prattled on and on about the game they were playing, gushing about this and that amazing and dramatic turn of events in the ongoing saga of their toys. This was something I usually only half listened to, but in that moment I found myself really appreciating their creativity—such elaborate storylines and character development! I looked them in the eye when they talked. I paid attention to what they were saying. I tried to just be there. Then I told them both how much I loved them, knelt down on the pink rug, kissed one, then the other on the head, and exited the playroom.

They were so precious to me. Thinking about how much I loved them sometimes made me feel like my heart wasn't quite big enough to contain it all. How often was I missing these moments to worry about my weight? They didn't care what weight I was. I doubted they would even notice if I gained 5 pounds, while I acted like the world was ending. They probably *did* notice when I was grumpy, distracted, or not present while they talked. I took some time to really think about how my obsession with food had overshadowed things in my life that were more important. I didn't want that to continue to be the case. It was time to make my thought life match my actual priorities.

So much of my mental energy was spent in the past, beating myself up for failures and reliving painful moments; or in the future, worrying over things that hadn't even happened yet. There was so much peace simply being in the moment.

I had also observed something amazing in this process, something that might be the key to this whole thing:

I told my brain to think some other thoughts and focus on some other things.

And it obeyed.

This was how I made *my* present more enjoyable, just like Aphrodite's. Sitting on my couch and thinking about all the things I was grateful for, I *felt* grateful. In the same way, when I thought about all the things I hated about my body, I *felt* hate. So, if I thought in ways that were loving, I could *feel* love, just like Aphrodite. I knew this had to be one of her secrets. If the main emotion she felt was love, no wonder she was happy all the time! I thought about the overwhelming love I felt for my daughters when I focused on them in their playroom and wondered if that was the amount of love she felt for herself. I couldn't even imagine what it would be like to carry around that level of overwhelming, heart bursting, love for oneself all the time. It seemed like too much.

Was it too much? Could she keep it inside? If you have so much love in you, does it spill out and wash over everyone around you? I could see how it would be easier to offer love to others if you had plenty to spare. I liked the idea of that, *having love to spare.*

Unfortunately, I also found I had trouble sustaining the practice of being present or directing my thoughts to love, gratitude, or anything for more than a few moments at a time. Once I left the playroom and went to start some laundry, the other Thoughts came back. I *had* been able to do it for a little while though, and I had felt relief during that time. I thought, *Hey, maybe I could get better at this. Maybe I could train myself to sustain other thoughts. Maybe I could learn to be present and not think of food outside of mealtimes. Maybe I could focus on feeling grateful.* It might be hard, but it would be worth it.

I committed my energy to the process of training my brain to be present. Throughout the day, whenever I could, I practiced thinking about only what was in front of me: making the bed, brushing my teeth, folding laundry, or doing dishes. I tried to give these things my full attention even though they were somewhat boring, just to practice. I noticed the texture and feel of the items in my hands, I noticed smells, I listened to the sounds in the room. I especially focused on significant moments during the day, like dinner with the family, all conversations, or goodnight hugs and kisses, tuning into the love I felt for the people in my life.

I started a mindfulness practice to help me on my way. I downloaded an app that walked you through the process of becoming fully present and committed to doing that 3 times a day for a month. Each session was 10-20 minutes.

It was *hard*.

My brain was all over the place.

I didn't want to sit still. I had other things to do and kept battling with the excuses that I didn't have time. I did it anyway.

When my mind wandered to the Thoughts I brought it back to my breath.

When it wandered again I brought it back again.

And again.

And again. It wasn't quick or easy, but I did get better.

I don't believe I will ever completely master the skill of being present. Learning to be in the present moment and think on purpose has been an ongoing practice that I am still growing in today, but I know it began that day. It started when I realized for that brief moment while hanging out in Aphrodite's head that my present could feel better. That I could direct my brain to think of things other than food or my body. That I could experience the joy of being fully present with the people in my life. I was nowhere near perfect or consistent with the process, but I continued to train myself to think of food and meals *only at mealtimes*.

The rest of the day, I genuinely worked to think about other things. One of the things I chose was gratitude. Specifically, each morning, I wrote in a gratitude journal.

It wasn't hard. I had so much to be grateful for. For once, I started to actually *feel* it.

Turns out, when my head was filled with grateful thoughts, there was a lot less room for body-hate.

Chapter 7

What Would Aphrodite Think about Hunger?

All right, so far I discovered that Aphrodite would have thought of other things when she wasn't eating. Cool. I had also seen that, with a little grit, I could also think of other things. Cool. For my next session with Aphrodite, I tried to imagine what would have happened between not eating and eating. *How would* that *process have gone for her?* For me, as soon as I felt hunger, I also felt panic. Not cool.

Oh, God. I'm hungry AGAIN! Should I eat? Should I not eat? How long has it been since I last ate? Only 3 hours?!?! That's not long enough! I need to minimize calories. I can't eat yet. This is so uncomfortable. I want it to go away. I don't want to gain wait. Maybe I can wait a little longer. I can ignore it.

Bottom line? I was afraid of eating because I was afraid of weight gain. Mostly I was afraid that if I started eating I wouldn't stop. I had a lot of evidence to validate that fear from my bulimic days. Even though I didn't purge my stomach these days, I did still binge eat from time to time. Also, I just overate fairly often, consuming more food than my body really needed, which I knew was a more acceptable form of disordered eating, but disordered nonetheless.

Typically after eating what I considered an appropriate amount of food, I didn't feel satiated at all. Sometimes I stopped anyway. Other times, I would continue to eat until my stomach was distended and uncomfortable and still want more, which made no sense!

I felt angry at myself for being weak and not being able to stop eating when I planned to. I felt angry at my body for continuing to ask for food, because that made it so much harder.

My body is betraying me. It is setting me up to fail. I always have to choose between being full and gaining weight or feeling hungry and being thin. It's not fair! What is wrong with my body? Why can't it just cooperate?

I needed some major help in this area. Back to the sofa for an Aphrodite session!

I started by tuning into the mind of a woman who loved her body. I tried to settle into that space.

I love this body. This body is perfect just the way it is. I have no need to change it.

Once I felt settled into Aphrodite's self-love, I tried to imagine her feeling hunger. I picked up with my earlier vision and imagined her back at the market with her basket. I watched her in my mind's eye, walking around the market, and tried to imagine what would happen when she recognized a hunger pang. I saw her reaching for a candle, then hesitating for just a moment as she registered the hunger. There was a gentle lifting of her head, chin slightly to the side, like she was considering something. I watched the change in her eyes as they shifted from focusing on the outside world to what was happening inside of her. It was so subtle. I nearly missed it. After that moment, she turned her attention back to shopping. Her face remained serene and open. There was no negative emotional response. She didn't panic. She wasn't angry at her body for being hungry. She just continued what she was doing.

I opened my eyes. This made sense. For her, eating food was not negative because she didn't need to lose weight, so the hunger that preceded eating wouldn't have been negative either. She loved her body just the way it was. No need to change it. No need to ignore hunger signals in order to restrict calories.

In the context of Aphrodite's perfect self-love, hunger would feel...neutral. Not good or bad. If she was not trying to change her body, hunger would just be hunger. No more. No less.

Lesson 2: Aphrodite views hunger as neutral.

This was my next exercise to try on myself. I wasn't hungry right then, so I checked on the kids, settled in at my computer to get caught up on emails, and waited for my opportunity to imitate Aphrodite. About an hour later, I was sitting at my desk when I felt a pang of hunger. When it registered, I tried not to think anything negative about the hunger itself or my body for feeling it. I breathed deeply and tried to settle into some peace and calm within myself alongside the hunger.

I thought neutral thoughts: *I am hungry. This is my body being hungry. This is what hunger feels like. This is my body asking for food.* Initially, I found that I still panicked, so I also added some comforting thoughts: *This is just hunger. This is okay. We're going to be fine. Hunger doesn't mean weight gain.*

In addition to giving myself this little speech when I felt hunger, I also accessed the memory of my session with Aphrodite. I re-watched her feeling hunger and not having an emotional response. I remembered her serene face. I latched on to her totally neutral emotions about her hunger, and tried to make my own emotions match. I tried to *feel* love for my body in the midst of feeling the (totally neutral) sensation of hunger. I relaxed my shoulders. I smoothed out the furrow in my brow. I gently lifted the corners of my mouth in a slight smile.

This is hunger.

I felt so much better! By viewing hunger as neutral, I could experience it, but still BREATHE. My chest wasn't so tight. I could take full, deep breaths. I was able to think without panic. I hadn't realized how negative and visceral of a reaction I had been having until it was gone.

As I took time to breathe and sit with the hunger, I could see how unfair it had been to be mad at my body for getting hungry. This was part of what it was designed to do.

This was a monumental shift for me. Hunger had been a lot of things during my life, but *neutral* was not one of them. When I was mired in anorexic seasons, hunger was a constant companion, the measuring stick by which I gauged my success. Its absence meant I had eaten too much food, and that was bad. I actually thought of hunger as a good sign, even though it felt terrible. When I was actively trying to lose weight, hunger was my weapon. It was how I punished myself after overeating. It was how I punished myself for being fat. When I was allowing everything, feeling hunger produced excitement and anticipation, because it meant I was going to go eat food—and probably a lot of it.

It took a lot of practice before hunger became a truly neutral experience for me.

I got hungry often though, so I practiced a lot too.

Chapter 8

What Would Aphrodite Do About Hunger?

The next question I needed to answer was whether Aphrodite would act on the feeling of hunger. I had to imagine she would. The only reason I ignored hunger and denied my body food was because I thought that's how I would lose weight.

Aphrodite would love her body right now, at the weight it was today. She would prize it. She would care for it.

So if she were hungry, I assumed she would eat.

Okay. I can do that too. Right? Maybe? Wait. Can I actually do that? I'm not really her. I'm hungry ALL THE TIME! If I eat every time I'm hungry I'm going to be the size of a house! (I took a brief interlude to spend some quality time going through a heart racing freak-out for a bit. You know how it is.)

Inhale. Hold. Release.

Inhale. Hold. Release.

I didn't want to do this, but I knew I would *have* to if I was going to act like Aphrodite. I knew I must. It was imperative that I figure out how to act lovingly towards my body, because I had to be able to show my girls how to love theirs. Someone who loved herself would eat when she was hungry.

I could do this. I *would* do this. Even if it was scary.

Even though I had my initial answer, I still took time to check in with Aphrodite before trying it out. I was learning that there was more to WWAD than what she actually did. I also wanted to see what she was thinking and feeling. I knew love would be present, but what else? I replayed the earlier visions of her going about her day, shopping at the market, and registering hunger with neutrality. Basic thought: *I'm hungry.* As I added on the mental decision to eat, I found that it was also neutral: *I'm hungry, so I will eat.*

No value judgements about her body. No judgements about herself. She wasn't calling herself weak. Hunger is a natural part of being human. All human bodies get hungry. All humans have to eat. Simple. Neutral.

And yet...

As I started to watch for when I was hungry, calming speech at the ready, I noticed something. There were actually two different pulls to eat. One was physical hunger. The other was the emotional desire to eat. I had been eating in response to both.

Would Aphrodite do that? Nope.

I knew this was the key. Aphrodite *would* eat when her body genuinely needed food for fuel; when it was physically hungry. That would be loving. She would *not* eat when her body didn't need food, even if she wanted it for other reasons. Putting food into her body that it didn't need wouldn't be loving.

Lesson 3: Aphrodite eats when she is physically hungry.

63

Initially, I struggled to tell the difference between the two. I just knew I wanted food. *How are you supposed to tell the difference?*

I started paying attention and discovered I felt physical hunger in my abdomen—like a hollowness right at the base of my ribcage. Emotional hunger often felt like a desire to chew.

Eventually, I learned that there were other pulls to eat food that had nothing to do with physical hunger or emotions, but involved more complicated processes in the body (insulin, blood sugar, glycemic index, fat adaptation, and more). Really understanding when my body needed fuel actually took years rather than months.

All throughout that process, I continued to apply my WWAD method and mimic loving my body no matter what.

I chose to label *all* the different pulls to eat as neutral.

I made decisions about when to eat based on what was best for my physical body. I thought of it as my most prized possession and considered what would be best for it, rather than what would be most comfortable for me in the moment.

I continued to mimic Aphrodite, even when I got it wrong and ate food for emotional rather than physical reasons.

I never denied my body food it needed for fuel out of anger, frustration, impatience, or a desire for it to be different.

I didn't deny my body food based on my weight.

I didn't deny my body food based on what I ate at a previous meal.

If I was physically hungry, I ate.

Simultaneously, I began to learn to manage the other pulls to eat without food, which made applying this lesson a whole lot easier!

Chapter 9

How Would Aphrodite Respond to Hunger?

Now, we entered a new stage of the process, one that I hadn't realized existed until that moment. It began at the decision to eat and ran until the food was actually in my body. This stretch of time could actually last a while depending on the situation. If I grabbed something that was pre-made or required no prep, the time spent in this stage was very short. Preparing a three course meal...different story.

When I decided I was going to allow myself to eat, I felt frenzied. I rushed to get the food in me as quickly as possible, often eating standing up in my kitchen. I think some of this was physical. You see, I typically didn't *let* myself eat until I was already quite hungry. *Too* hungry. By then, I felt like I was starving. I think most of it was emotional though. I craved the numbness that came from eating but dreaded the guilt that came after. I resisted as long as I could, but once I caved and decided I would eat, I was like an addict racing for the next fix with single-minded determination. This whole stage from the decision to eat food until I actually ate felt terrible. Another stark contrast from Aphrodite. All of this was born out of my past restricting, overeating, and dieting mentality. This was not part of the equation for a woman who loved herself.

I returned to my vision of Aphrodite and watched her in my mind's eye to see how she would respond. I was shocked to see that even once she decided to eat, nothing changed immediately. She was in the middle of her shopping and merely continued the task. She wasn't denying her body food like I did. There were no thoughts of deprivation or denial. She wasn't angry about being hungry. She was *totally* going to eat, and likely soon, she just wasn't rushing to get there. She finished her task with only a small bit of her awareness on her hunger and looked totally at ease while doing it. When she was finished, she calmly went to find food.

Lesson 4: Aphrodite responds to hunger calmly.

I opened my eyes and just sat there on my couch, confused by the outcome of the session. *How was she so calm? How was that even possible?* I held the image of her in my mind and just pondered her and what I knew. For starters, she would never have starved herself, because that isn't loving. Food would always have been an option, always available. It was never forbidden, never denied. So, she may never have gotten as crazy-hungry as I often did. That would have helped, but even if she was completely famished for some reason outside of her control, the physical discomfort would have come with the knowledge that she would always be allowed to eat as much as her body needed once it was available.

Eating is always allowed.

So many of my fears came from feeling like every meal might be my last *real* one. I was perpetually on the verge of going on a diet. I was constantly planning to go on one "soon." Because the good food might be going away soon, it made sense to stock up beforehand. Enjoy it while I could. Live while I was able. It was always feast or famine. For Aphrodite it was neither.

Her love for her body was constant.

I committed to putting this into practice in conjunction with the last two lessons. The next time I felt hungry, I spoke calmly to myself: *I feel hungry and I will eat soon.* I didn't drop everything and race to the kitchen. I tried to keep calm and take deep breaths. I told myself things like: *I'm okay. I'm allowed to eat. The food won't go away. I can have food whenever I am truly hungry. I can eat as much as my body needs. I love this body. I care for this body. It's going to be fine.*

If it was nearly family meal time, it sometimes made sense to just wait a little bit and patiently sit with the hunger. If it was it was going to be several hours before the rest of the family would eat again, I chose to eat then. Regardless of the length of time, moving from panicked urgency to calm during these times was transforming huge chunks of my day…and Aphrodite and I hadn't even gotten to the actual eating yet!

The anxiety still came up sometimes. When it did, I just talked myself through it, trying to see if I could generate the same kind of feelings that Aphrodite would have felt. I tried to put myself in her headspace, one of love and one without a history of starvation.

Regardless of what I was feeling, I still tried to act the way she would have while feeling hunger. I kept up my "hunger is neutral" script in my mind. I spoke calmly to my family. I took slow, deep breaths. I finished tasks first. I made my body move at an unhurried pace when I was getting the food ready. I forced myself to be present with the preparations and go through the steps with serenity.

I told myself not to panic. And myself listened.

I learned a very valuable lesson. Hunger does *not* produce emotions. Hunger is only a physical sensation. I get to decide what emotion comes after. I had been choosing panic, but I could choose peace.

I liked peace much better.

Chapter 10

What Would Aphrodite Eat?

I "scheduled" my next session with Aphrodite fairly soon, because once I felt hunger, decided I would eat, and calmly went to the kitchen, I still had to decide *what* to eat. This was the one I had been waiting for. The main event. I had been patient. I had worked through the process and did my homework so that I could approach this moment from the right headspace. I was done waiting. It was time! Even more than the normal urgency to figure out the "right" thing to do, I found I was *so* curious to see what Aphrodite's answer was. Lord knows I didn't have one. Or, perhaps more accurately, I had too many answers.

I knew all the methods. I knew all of the information. I could tell you about a variety of diets that were considered healthy. I knew how to eat for inflammation, leaky gut, and autoimmunity. I knew how to eat to lose weight. I knew how to eat to build muscle. But, I was completely clueless on how to eat in order to love my body. Or, in Aphrodite's case, how to eat if you already loved your body.

I actually had a number of food restrictions for my health condition that I had to follow to maintain my current, improved state of health. Even within those bounds, my food choices and portions were still primarily governed by my desire to be thin. When I looked at food, I asked myself, "Will this make me fat?"

What would Aphrodite ask herself? What questions would guide her as she chose what to put into her body? I was so curious to see what she would have thought, and felt, and chosen. So, right there in my kitchen, I leaned against the cool, granite counter and shut my eyes.

I started by replaying the visions from my prior sessions with Aphrodite. Then, I pictured Aphrodite standing in my kitchen, peeking into my fridge. I waited with bated breath to see what she would think and feel and do. She perused the options, and asked herself, *What would nourish my body?* I opened my eyes and just took that in for a minute.

Nourish. What a word. I did a quick Google for the definition. This is what popped up: *to provide with food or other substances necessary for growth, health, and good condition.*

Aphrodite's body was her fame, a prized possession. She would have cared for it. She would have provided it with the food necessary to keep it in good working condition. She would have eaten the most nourishing food available.

While my body wasn't the source of any sort of fame or accolades, it still needed care. It was the only one I had. I was a Mom and I couldn't parent well if my body wasn't functioning well, something I knew well from the years I spent bed-bound. I also believe in serving others and making a difference in the world. I had never thought about how important a nourished body was for such things. It is hard to do much with your body if it isn't in good condition.

Lesson 5: Aphrodite chooses nourishing foods to eat.

So, *Which foods are nourishing?* I pondered all the foods that I knew about and tried to picture the most nourishing ones. I pictured colorful fruits and vegetables, living plants that were full of vitamins and nutrients. I pictured foods that were whole and unprocessed, looking very similar to the way they grew in nature. I pictured foods that were *real* foods. I was totally comfortable with *this* aspect of nourishing.

As I thought about what made a food nourishing, I realized another key aspect was the concentration of nutrition. The more packed-in the goodness, the more nourishing the food. This realization brought me face to face with high calorie, high fat foods, which I was decidedly less comfortable with. (Things like olive oil, coconut, avocado, and nuts.)

Many high fat, high calorie foods are *very* nourishing to the body. I wasn't confused about fat...theoretically. Despite being raised in the low-fat craze of the 90's, I knew the claims that fat makes you fat had been completely debunked. I had also learned that weight gain and loss was about much more than calorie content. The problem was, if I ate highly concentrated foods, I didn't need as much of it. For me, the quantity had always been decidedly more important than quality.

I had wanted to be able to eat the most possible food and not gain weight. That for me meant a lot of high-volume, low-calorie, low-nutrition foods. Things like rice cakes or popcorn. I'm not saying either are bad, but I am saying I only ate them because they had very little actual substance, meaning I could nibble and crunch on them for a long while. Neither would be things I would choose if I was actually searching for what would be most nourishing.

I know enough about nutrition to know that there are plenty of "gray area" foods out there. I personally have certain foods that I cannot eat due to my various health conditions that would be perfectly fine for someone else. Aphrodite and me selecting nourishing foods was not about creating a definitive list for the entire planet to follow, it was about me making good choices based on what I did know and based on my own body. Mostly, it was about releasing the parameters of weight loss when making those decisions and replacing them with the parameters of love.

Aphrodite ate in order to love and care for her body, choosing nourishing foods. I got that. When I thought about the food in our house, I realized most of it was nourishing. My daughter's food allergies and my genetic condition prevented us from being able to eat a lot of the more traditional junk food out there.

With so many nourishing foods available, What Would Aphrodite Do? How would she choose?

It was simple and profound. I thought that she would eat what she wanted at the moment. Perhaps what sounded good to her was actually what her body needed, or maybe it would be nothing more than her personal preference among a group of nourishing options. Would that be so bad though? If you've got to pick between a bunch of great options, why not pick the one you want?

The main reason I didn't eat what I wanted was because I did not trust myself or my body. Eating food I didn't enjoy helped ensure I wouldn't eat too much of it—though I often felt unsatisfied after. (You don't get very satisfied with un-nourishing food you don't even want.)

Aphrodite would have trusted her body, its signals, and her own desires within the bounds of loving choices. I didn't interpret this to be the same thing as following and indulging every craving. If Aphrodite felt a craving for something she knew would be harmful, I assume she wouldn't have responded. If I had a strong urge to drink dish soap, I wouldn't do that, even if it sounded good. That wouldn't be loving or nourishing. If she wanted one nourishing food over another though, I believe she would have trusted her desires.

I recounted scores of times in my life when I had refused to eat what I really wanted for one reason or another. I am typically a chocolate and caramel kind of girl over anything fruity, but I remember going to a frozen custard place for dessert in college (during a season of everything-allowed-mode) and really wanting a sundae with strawberries and marshmallow cream. However, I *made* myself get the one with a big brownie, chocolate, and caramel because that was a "real" dessert. In my mind, fruit was "healthy," and therefore could not serve as my indulgent treat.

I have fixed food for myself, taken a bite, realized it didn't really taste as good as I thought it would, and eaten it anyway so that it wouldn't be wasted. I've eaten what was convenient but unappealing over what sounded good but would take more time to make. I have eaten an entire plate full of veggies when all I really wanted was a little meat, simply because the plate of veggies was lower calorie and allowed me to eat more.

Shortly before I got to this lesson with Aphrodite, I was eating lunch with my daughters. I was having a salad with black olives on it. My kids had the olives, protein, and veggies deconstructed and sans the leafy greens. Rather than using a fork, they were putting the olives on their fingers, growling like monsters with misshapen claws, and then eating them— hey, whatever works. They kept talking about how much they *loved* olives. I told them how, when I was a kid, I didn't like olives, even though the rest of my family did. They asked, "But you like them now?" I opened my mouth to answer... then shut it again.

The truth was that I didn't really *know* if I liked them or not. I hadn't really thought much about it. I speared one, put it in my mouth, and really tasted it. Nope, I still didn't really like olives! I didn't hate them, but at that moment, they actually didn't sound appealing at all. I bought them and served them to myself because I had read that they were very good for you. If I was to eat like Aphrodite, then black olives would be out unless my taste changed. They were nourishing, but I didn't like them.

This was a lot to take in. Thinking this way would require a completely different way of approaching food choices. Now, standing in my kitchen, I was supposed to actually choose a meal option based on love, nourishment, and what I wanted. That was just crazy town as far as I was concerned, but Aphrodite wasn't phased. I am really thankful that I am a naturally tenacious person, otherwise I may have bailed before this next step, where we went from visions, theory, and emotions to real action.

I gripped the refrigerator handle, took a deep breath to steady myself, and calmly pulled open the door. As the cool air hit my face, I did exactly what I saw Aphrodite do in my vision. I scanned the shelves and asked myself: *What would nourish my body? What could I eat to show my body love? What sounds good?*

I picked some raw spinach I had just bought at the farmer's market, because it was the brightest thing in there and I knew greens had lots of amazing nutrients. I also grabbed some eggs and a ripe avocado. I fried the eggs—allowing myself 3 instead of my usual 2—put them on top of the greens, and added the sliced avocado to the top. Most of the time, I limited how much avocado I allowed myself to have due to the high calorie content. For this meal, I added twice that amount because I knew it really was a super nourishing food. My brain panicked a little as it began to automatically calculate calories, but I shut that down and just kept talking myself through it and directing my brain to more positive thoughts: *This food will nourish my body. This is how I care for my body. This is loving.*

I carried my plate to the dining room and sat at the table. I was gloriously alone due to the odd time of day I was eating—a very intentional choice to give me uninterrupted time for what I was doing—and was immediately faced with my next question.

Chapter 11

How Would Aphrodite Eat?

Sitting at my dining room table, with a nourishing plate of food in front of me, I now had to figure out: *How would Aphrodite eat? How does one eat a meal if they love their body just the way it is?* I had never thought of such a thing. I typically ate too fast to think about much of anything except getting the food in me without violating basic table etiquette. I knew how to eat in ways that were socially acceptable—not chewing with my mouth open or talking with food in my mouth—but I had no idea how to eat from a place of love.

What Would Aphrodite Do? How would she go about the physical act of eating? I was already in her headspace from the previous exercise, so I just popped back over to my vision of her. This time, I imagined her at my table with this exact meal in front of her and "watched" to see what she did.

The first thing I noticed as she picked up her fork and took her first bite was that she ate *calmly*. Slowly. She didn't rush. She didn't scarf down her food. I saw her take bites that were neither too big or too small and chew them thoroughly. At one point she sat her fork down while chewing, looked out the window that was to the left of the table, and didn't seem like she was in a huge hurry to pick it back up. She seemed so… relaxed. Chill. Carefree. Nonchalant. It was just food. Just a meal.

She seemed to enjoy what she was eating, but wasn't rushing to get more of it in her body. She was taking the time to really savor it. *Ha. I couldn't have been more different.* I thought I enjoyed the food I ate, but I didn't enjoy it the way she did. Half the time I barely tasted it because I was shoveling it in so fast. I enjoyed the feeling of food in me, but my enjoyment had very little to do with the actual eating. Watching Aphrodite eat, I was witnessing true enjoyment. The enjoyment that comes from really tasting.

I opened my eyes and took a calming breath. I tried to continue to embody Aphrodite with my eyes open. I tried to really *be* her in that moment while in my body. I would have to if I was going to get through this. *I am a woman who loves herself and am sitting down to a nourishing meal.* I reached down and picked up my fork, feeling the cool metal in my hand. I speared some egg, avocado, and greens with my fork. I raised it to my mouth and took my first bite. It hit my tongue, a mix of warm eggs, cool spinach, and creamy avocado. I chewed slowly and thoroughly, noticing the mix of firm vegetable matter contrasted with the soft eggs and avocado. I noticed how the three flavors blended into a synergistic whole. Then, when it was chewed to small enough bits, I swallowed.

That was an interestingly focused bite, but now what? *Hey Aphrodite, what do we think about while we eat food?*

She would continue to think about her food and eating, because that is what was currently happening and it wasn't something she needed to avoid for any reason. Ergo, be present. So, I thought about my food more, noticing differences from one bite to another. I forced myself to continue to chew slowly, which was an act of will—I hadn't realized how fast I typically ate! At one point, I started to get really distracted, so I sat my fork down on the table for a minute and took a little break, partly to prove to myself I could. *The food isn't going anywhere. It will be here when you're ready.*

I imagined what else Aphrodite might think during a meal: *I love this body. This food is so good for me. This is nourishing my body. This is such a caring thing to do for my body. This food is delicious. I am so grateful that we have enough food to eat. I am grateful that I have a functional human stomach that can digest food.*

The whole process felt...reverent. For a woman who loved herself, eating was a meaningful act, rather than the mindless frenzy I was familiar with. Sitting down to a meal was something done to tangibly demonstrate the love and respect that was already felt. While I sat there trying to be her, I did feel it. Not only as her, I was able to experience some of the gratitude as *myself.* My body wasn't perfect, but there were always things to be grateful for if I looked for them. I was definitely grateful that putting food on the table wasn't a struggle. I was grateful for access to quality food. I was grateful that I had a body that could digest solid food (something that wasn't always true for me).

Lesson 6: Aphrodite eats as an act of love.

I have heard people say, "Food is fuel." I think there is a lot of truth to that. Food does fuel us. That is its primary purpose. Seeing food as a fuel source for the body could definitely help a person make good food choices. It would also eliminate using food as a way to manage emotions or as a form of entertainment.

Aphrodite's love for herself was a new layer, a deeper perspective. Eating food was *more* than just fueling my body.

Much more. It wasn't just a clinical calculation of how to fulfill daily nutritional requirements. It was loving my body.

My eating used to be a reflection of my self-loathing.

Moving forward, it would a declaration of my love.

Chapter 12

When Would Aphrodite Stop Eating?

Before picking up my fork and continuing my meal, I needed to answer the question, "When would Aphrodite *stop* eating?" I was about half-way done and needed to figure it out before I went further. Sitting at my dining table, fully embodying Aphrodite, the answer was simple. I didn't even have to visualize her: *Stop when you are satisfied.* Not after you are bloated, stuffed, and feel terribly uncomfortable. Not while you are still hungry. Stop when you have had *just enough.*

I had heard this dozens of times. It was a main theme of every diet book and all the weight loss advice I had ever read. I had simply never been able to actually *do* it. Every time I got to the place of being physically satisfied and told myself I was *supposed* to stop when I was satisfied, that I really *should* do that, I turned into a petulant child and did the opposite. I resented the idea of stopping when satisfied. Eating felt good while I was doing it, and good feelings were still pretty rare. I didn't want that to be taken away. When I stopped eating, I would have to go back to feeling all the things I didn't want to feel. So, I kept eating, felt temporarily numbed, then felt even worse when I came back to reality because now I had the guilt of overeating to deal with as well.

Aphrodite absolutely would have stopped when she was satisfied, but for a completely different reason. Not in order to lose weight or even to keep from gaining weight. She would have stopped because she loved and respected herself too much to overeat. Overeating is hard on the digestive system. So, doing it wouldn't be loving. It would be the opposite of caring for her body. It really doesn't feel good either. I knew that. Never, ever had I overeaten and then thought, "Wow, this feels awesome!" It doesn't. It is genuinely uncomfortable.

If, like Aphrodite, I was allowed to eat again whenever I was hungry, there would be no need to overeat now. There was no impending diet to prepare for, just a future filled with loving choices.

I began checking in with my hunger after each bite, before getting another. When I had two bites left on my plate, I was pretty sure I felt satisfied. I was no longer hungry, but I didn't feel uncomfortably full either. I sat my fork down on my plate and stared at the two remaining bites. It was not easy to imagine throwing them out. *That's wasteful. You can't throw away food. There are starving children somewhere in Africa! It's just two bites. It would be better to just eat it.* I was tempted to listen. These thoughts seemed very practical and logical. Was I more interested in logic or love? Is eating food I don't need in order to not waste it loving? I didn't think so. Eating those two bites wouldn't feed anyone else who was hungry, it would just hurt me. I did learn it would be better to make a little less next time, knowing I could always get more.

For this meal, I needed to just be done. I kept up a steady stream of thoughts as I talked myself through it, *You can eat more as soon as you are hungry. This is what love looks like right now. We want to care for this body and that means not overeating. Overeating feels terrible and you don't really want to do that.*

81

I carried my plate to the trash, stepped on the lever, and scraped the two remaining bites into the bin. I loaded my dishes in the dishwasher and went to start my afternoon work. My hunger felt satiated and I was really proud of myself. There was a little bit of fear about getting hungry again soon. *If I get hungry, I can eat again. No big deal.*

Lesson 7: Aphrodite stops eating when she is satisfied.

I really tried to make this my new standard. It didn't always happen. Sometimes, I was rushing or distracted and would eat past my satisfied point before realizing it.

When I took the time to first visualize myself as Aphrodite— her loving thoughts and feelings—and to remind myself *why* I didn't want to overeat, stopping was easy.

To stop eating as a punishment felt awful and was something I had rebelled against.

To stop eating out of love felt…well…

…loving.

Chapter 13

What Wouldn't Aphrodite Eat?

I really connected with the idea of choosing foods that were nourishing. It made perfect sense to me. I found that this general guideline covered most of my questions in terms of food choices. I would simply look at the food available at the store and ask myself, *What would nourish my body?* And I bought that. I would look at the foods in my home and ask myself, *What sounds good?* And I ate that. My mental energy was focused on finding nourishing foods and listening to my body to eat the ones that sounded good. My food mantra was: *I eat foods that are nourishing*. Pretty simple.

I initially didn't think too much about the *other* foods—the ones I wasn't buying or eating because I didn't consider them nourishing. I was mostly home, by myself, and it didn't come up right away. Eventually I knew I would have to ask Aphrodite about those as well, because I really didn't know what to think.

I got my chance a few weeks later. I was at an event with a group of other moms, something we did monthly. After greeting and mingling with the other ladies for a bit, I made my way over to the food table. There were lots of packaged snacks, cookies, and desserts along with some veggies and dip. Aphrodite and I would have to work with the food in front of us. Thankfully, I was getting much more comfortable with our work together, because a group gathering doesn't exactly offer the option of sitting quietly with your eyes closed when it is time to eat!

At past events, I often didn't eat the desserts, sticking with fruits and veggies. I would get a lot of comments about how "good" I was for eating healthy, but I mostly just felt like I was missing out. I wasn't allowed to eat those foods because of the special diet I needed to be on for my health. True, I needed to adjust my diet to stay out of that wheelchair, but honestly, I was *glad* to have the excuse to avoid the desserts so I wouldn't get any pudgier. As I watched thin ladies load their plates with desserts I bemoaned how unfair it all was.

This isn't fair. I wish I could have that, but I'm *not allowed.*

This night was so different. I looked at the spread and asked, *What Would Aphrodite Do? What is nourishing? How would she love her body and herself if she was in this exact situation?* I specifically pondered the desserts. They certainly weren't nourishing, but did that mean they were off limits? Were food restrictions loving? I've heard they are a bad idea. I've heard that we shouldn't restrict ourselves or it will lead to bingeing later on. That it is better to allow all things in moderation. *I mean, isn't it loving to treat yourself sometimes!?*

Every dieter I had ever seen would "be good" for a period of time and then treat themselves to some indulgent food that wasn't part of the diet as a reward for avoiding it the rest of the week. Desserts were forbidden when dieting, and they were a reward for being thin.

Aphrodite didn't diet though. She loved her body just the way it was. So desserts would not have been off limits for the purpose of weight loss. Did that mean Aphrodite *would* eat these things even though they *weren't* nourishing?

I stood at the food table with my eyes wide open, appearing to just be checking the spread, while actually working to embody

Aphrodite. I pulled myself out of that dieter mentality and into the mind of Aphrodite that was motivated by pure love. I imagined Aphrodite's loving herself and her body completely and how that would feel. I tuned into her thoughts about her body—that it was perfect and something she wanted to care for and nourish. As I looked at the desserts, I tried to connect with Aphrodite's thoughts and asked for her wisdom and guidance to know what was truly loving in this situation. I waited for a moment, then this is sentence ran through my mind:

I love myself too much to eat that.

Holy Crap. Mind. Blown. Yes! Of course! It all came back to loving this body and making decisions that reflected that love. Processed, packaged, sugar-filled, non-food treats would *not* be loving. There was nothing nourishing about them. They had calories, but very little actual nutrition. Plus, many of them were filled with harmful things. For a woman who loved herself, the decision of whether to eat them or not would have *nothing* to do with weight and everything to do with kindness.

I think I could have stood there and just absorbed that concept for a long time, but I didn't want to be awkward. So, I grabbed some veggies—which I actually wanted—and I walked away from the desserts not feeling the least bit deprived.

Lesson 8: Aphrodite doesn't put harmful things into her body.

Later, at home, I spent time pondering all of this more. I thought about all the foods that I had chosen not to eat in the past. My reason for avoiding foods had generally been to not gain weight. If I was trying to lose weight, I had restrictions. If I wasn't trying to lose weight, I didn't have restrictions. Restrictions were all about weight loss to me. The only reason I could fathom skipping dessert was weight loss.

Once again, Aphrodite did things a little different. If I was acting like her, then I would no longer be worried about my weight, so that wasn't a factor. I would love my body just as it was, but I would also prize my body and want to care for it. In that context, would there be foods that I didn't eat for other reasons?

My first thought was of my firstborn, Zoe. She was born with a life threatening dairy allergy. For her, eating dairy would be fatal, so definitely not loving and also not tied to weight loss. That is an extreme example, but lots of people have foods that they are allergic to, albeit less severely. Others have food intolerances or sensitivities. Most people at least know of foods that don't digest well for them. Yet, I have so many recollections of people saying things like, "I'm lactose intolerant, but I still eat ice cream because it's my favorite food!" or "I've got celiac, but I'm not going to miss out on birthday cake!" or just the general, "I know this is bad for me, but I'm going to eat it anyway!" This is pretty "normal" behavior from what I've observed and I have done the same myself. *I know I shouldn't, but I'm going to anyway!*

Something about that had always *felt* loving. Many women do this as a way to say, "I'm going to put weight loss aside for a minute and just love myself." *Would Aphrodite do that? Is that truly loving? Would she eat a food as a treat when she knew it hurt her body? Would it matter if it was a big hurt or a small hurt?*

No need to do a visualization on this one. Clearly not. No way. Not a chance. It wouldn't be loving. It wouldn't be nourishing. It would be harmful, and Aphrodite was teaching me that we don't harm things we truly love. Because she loved herself so completely, there would absolutely have been foods she chose not to eat, foods that she "restricted," but it would have been from love. This was fundamentally different from when I restricted foods from self-loathing or a desire to change my body. It changed everything.

So, if it was a question of whether a food was loving or harmful, I had an entirely different list of what to eat and not eat. I could think of a lot of foods that were harmful to the body completely separate from the concept of weight gain or loss. My brain started going through all the information I had come across in my life.

I'll be the first to admit that there is a lot of conflicting information out there in regard to food in general, not to mention that each unique body will have different needs. I think that is a secondary issue. I think the real issue is that so many of us don't live in accordance with the knowledge we *do* have. We *know* certain things aren't good for us, but we eat them anyway. We willfully and knowingly harm our bodies and half the time we brag about it! I had never really understood this so clearly until now. In the past, I hadn't been thinking about food in terms of love or harm; I had been thinking about weight gain or loss, or sometimes about managing health symptoms, but never about love.

When I thought about foods that one might not eat from love, the first thing that came to mind were edible non-food items. The truth is that there are a lot of products sold as food that have very little real food in them or contain the addition of non-food items—fillers, preservatives, dyes, and other chemicals that are harmful to the body, disrupt hormones, and increase the risk of cancer (among other nefarious things). Putting those things in my body would not be kind.

Eating non-food is not loving.

Similarly, many foods on the market are highly processed, scarcely resemble their natural food source, and lack any real nutrition. I am convinced Aphrodite, were she living today, would eat real food and avoid processed alternatives. There is just no way she would put something in her body with little or no nutritional value, because that's the opposite of nourishing!

One thing I had known for a long while was that refined, white sugar reacts in the body like a poison. It is a neurotoxin, a leading cause of cancer, messes with metabolism, is inflammatory, and a bunch of other stuff that was bad news for my body. Yet, despite knowing this for years, I still ate it anytime I wasn't trying to lose weight, or anytime I fell off the wagon of dieting. The only reason I had ever chosen to avoid sugar was for weight loss, but only because I had to. I loved the stuff. The very idea of removing sugar from my diet completely scared me to the point of near panic. Yet, I knew of no other food that was as harmful or had as little nutritional value as white sugar.

If Aphrodite and I were choosing only nourishing foods and avoiding putting harmful things in our bodies, then white sugar was perhaps the one food that was absolutely out. I am convinced that Aphrodite would have loved her body too much to feed it sugar. In that context, for the first time, removing sugar from my diet made sense to me and wasn't scary.

I love myself too much to put that in my body.

I was familiar with the concept of emotional eating, but never before had I seen it so clearly. The reasons that drove me to eat white sugar or other highly processed items had nothing to do with fueling or nourishing my physical body. That never even crossed my mind. I am convinced that is pretty true for almost everyone with even the most basic knowledge of nutrition. I mean, never ever has a doctor looked at a patient and said, "What you really need is more processed sugar.".

If I was eating a food that did not fuel or nourish my body in any way, then I was using it incorrectly. I was using it for something it was never meant for—like managing emotions. Food isn't for emotional management and using it for that was harming me. I realized that, scary as it was, maybe it was time I learned to handle those things properly, without food.

As I continued thinking in terms of actual, specific foods, I realized Aphrodite may have avoided many of the exact same things as I had avoided when dieting. For example, at Italian restaurants I often ate salad instead of pasta to reduce calories. She may have eaten that exact same salad because she loved herself—fresh, green, living things are probably the most nourishing things on the menu in many of those restaurants.

Why we DO or DON'T DO things matters. Avoiding a food isn't good or bad by itself. When I did it from self-loathing and hate it was truly unkind, but avoiding the exact same foods from love transformed it into an act of kindness.

I love myself too much to eat that.

Wow.

With this new standard, making food choices became so much easier. I could walk away from foods that I enjoyed the taste of, but that I knew didn't react well in my body, without feeling deprived. I didn't feel bad when I restricted harmful foods, no matter how tasty.

I felt proud.

I felt empowered.

I felt loved, cherished, prized, and cared for by my own food choices.

Saying no to harmful foods was easy for Aphrodite, and growing easier for me. Even I, who had always struggled to make good choices when it came to food, could see how much better this felt.

Just to be clear, in case you were getting the wrong idea: Sugar withdrawal sucks. Like, really, really sucks. Sugar is more addictive than cocaine and I went through genuine withdrawal when I removed it entirely. It was uncomfortable on a physical level: fatigue, headaches, brain fog, and generally feeling like I had the flu. It was even more uncomfortable on an emotional level: feeling sad without it, feeling powerful cravings to eat it, and learning to deal with my life without my go-to comfort food. It was genuinely hard in so many ways, but, think of it like getting a shot or having surgery. You go into it knowing it is going to feel bad. You know it is going to hurt, but it is the right and loving thing to do. It is what you need, so you do it anyway. This is just like that. Uncomfortable, but loving.

I'm so glad I gave it up.

Let me tell you this from the other side, being addicted to sugar sucks more than the withdrawal! Eating sugar felt good in the moment, but I was a slave to it. Completely and totally at its mercy. I had been since I was a kid. I remember waiting until my mom left the house and then sneaking into the kitchen and eating spoonfuls of brown sugar straight from the bag. (Yeah, like that kind of addicted. Don't judge. Or do. It's fine.)

Once I stopped eating sugar altogether, I realized that it had been majorly affecting my brain health. It contributed to depression, anxiety, and my obsessive, cyclical thinking. I just hadn't realized sugar was the culprit until it was gone for long enough. Sometimes it is like that with food. We don't really know something is harming us until we go without it for a while. Only then do we start to see how it is affecting us. The body is miraculous and will compensate for a lot to keep functioning. That doesn't mean it's loving to force it to.

After being completely sugar free for about a year we found a vegan, gluten-free bakery, which meant it was safe for Zoe, even with her dairy allergy. They mostly used natural sweeteners, but there was also some cane sugar as well. It was Zoe's birthday and we wanted to do something special. So, I decided a little sugar was fine as a "special treat."

Behind the curved glass, the display was filled with gorgeous treats. Beautifully decorated donuts, cupcakes, cookies, and more. I chose a cupcake, swirled high with pink frosting. I sat down in the wire chair in the outside eating area, and was thoroughly present. I enjoyed it and savored every bit of goodness. I took my time and stretched it out for several minutes, sipping my bitter coffee in between bites to reset my palate from the overload of sweet, which I was less accustomed to these days.

It. Tasted. Awesome.

By the time we made it home, I felt moody. Zoe and Nadia started arguing and I yelled at them until they were both crying. (THIS WAS NOT NORMAL FOR US.)

I woke the next morning with puffy eyes and feeling extra tired. All day my brain was a bit foggy. I felt sad and low starting my day. My *perfect husband was getting on my nerves. (*Did I mention he's helping edit this?) All in all, I felt off for three days. I was shocked. This was major. At first I thought it was just a coincidence, so I waited a month and went back to the bakery for another special treat and had the same result. Apparently, I *really* didn't do well with sugar. Seeing the fallout, I decided it was not worth the five minutes of sweetness.

I wish I could tell you that I was totally cured of any lingering desire for sugar after that, but I wasn't. It actually took a few more times of having treats on various holidays that were *mostly* nourishing, but contained just a *bit* of sugar, then feeling crummy afterwards before I finally and truly decided I was done.

I don't think of sugar as a "treat" anymore.

Feeling crummy isn't a treat…or a fun way to celebrate anything.

I still don't say, "I can never have it again." That is so dramatic. I tell myself the truth: *Of course* I can have sugar again…if I ever want to. The question is, do I truly want it?

For about a year after deciding sugar was not loving, every time I would be somewhere that a sugary treat was available, I would ask myself, *Do I want this?*

More specifically, *Do I want this and everything that comes with it? Do I have time for a headache later this afternoon? Can I do my work as well later with brain fog? Do I want to deal with 3 days of sugar cravings? Do I feel up to the task of managing a mind that is unruly? Do I have time for an emotional meltdown this evening? Would today be a good today to snap at my husband and kids?*

You know what? The answer has always been, "No." I never want those things. So, I never eat sugar. It is so much easier to not eat it than to deal with the consequences. I simply don't put it in my mouth.

I can honestly tell you this: today, I do not *like* sugar. I do not *want* sugar. Never ever again, even though I am allowed to and can do that without judgement. I just don't. I have occasionally eaten it by accident from not reading a condiment label or being given the wrong coffee order and I don't freak out about it. I don't beat myself up about it. I didn't "cheat."

I'm not off the wagon. This isn't a diet. I simply never intentionally choose things that have sugar in them and I stop eating something if I realize it does. I do not feel restricted by that. I'm not sad about it.

Sugar is harmful and I'm not a person who harms herself anymore. I have all my memories of how good it tastes and I still don't want it. I still don't like it in my body.

Dear reader, *this* is true freedom. We think freedom means eating whatever we want whenever we want it, but I was not free when I was addicted to sugar. I was ruled by my addiction. Now, I have the freedom to eat it or not eat it. I have the freedom to walk away without emotional backlash. I am truly free because I can actually say, "no." If you don't feel like you can go without it, then you are not free.

Eventually, sugar and other non-nourishing foods that had been major draws before, started to not even look appetizing. My brain screamed "harmful!" when I saw them.

So many people in my life assume that I feel deprived and restricted all the time because of the foods I don't eat. They couldn't be more wrong. I'm not using willpower to avoid those foods. When I focused on loving my body, I genuinely lost desire for them.

Think about it. If there is a food you don't like, then it is super easy to not eat it. Personally, I do not like the taste of mustard. It makes me gag unless it is heavily diluted with other flavors. I feel no need to apologize or justify to the world that I don't eat it. I don't feel proud of myself if I go 30 days without it. I don't make "90-Day No Mustard Challenges." I don't give myself reward after a week of avoiding the yellow stuff. I simply don't like it, so I don't eat it. That is how I feel about fast food, junk food, and sugar. That is how I now think and feel about the foods I restrict from love.

I don't like them. I don't want them. So, I don't eat them.

Every food I put in my mouth will either help or harm my body. I've learned there are varying degrees of help and harm to consider. I am constantly learning from the latest research and my own body about what works well for me in each new season. I don't claim to know everything there is to know about nutrition. I *am* consciously aware that every choice has consequences and I am 100% in control of what I choose.

I choose love.

And loving looks like not eating harmful foods.

Chapter 14

Where Would Aphrodite Find Joy?

One day, after eating my lunch, I was standing at my kitchen counter and eating a nourishing little chocolatey dessert I had whipped up. I felt good about choosing quality ingredients, but also curious. I tuned into my thoughts to see what I was thinking, not about the nourishment of the ingredients, but about the dessert itself. As I scooped up a bit, spoon gently scraping the side of the bowl, my thoughts were: *This is just for me. I deserve this. I need a little longer break. I'm not ready to go back to work yet. I'm tired. I need some energy. This will make me feel better. This is 'me time.'*

Oops.

Initially, my choice to avoid sugar or harmful foods equated to replacing ingredients. I was still eating desserts and treats as often as before, just better versions. I was having treats multiple times a day. I always wanted something sweet after a meal. I also typically took at least one break between lunch and dinner for a snack, which was often very dessert-like (don't forget the bedtime snacks).

Despite eating more nourishing version of dessert, I was still using food for something that it wasn't meant for. I was using it as a reward system, a reason for a break, an energy boost, and a nice little way to treat myself.

I took a minute to really check in with my body and noticed I wasn't actually hungry anymore. It just felt *wrong* somehow to go back to work without "a little something sweet." *This is my reward for having a well-balanced meal!*

Is that how Aphrodite would see it?

I learned to equate food with love, joy, happiness, fun, entertainment and celebration from my mom and other adults in my life when I was a child. If we won a softball game, we celebrated with ice cream. If my mom, older sister, and I had girl time, it involved eating out—probably at the Chinese buffet in the next town over. Snowy Sunday afternoons in the winter were for baking treats and watching Lifetime movies. My mom often encouraged me to bake my dad brownies so he would know I loved him. It was just what we did. Fun and food—especially sweet foods—always went together. I think that was part of why taking them away in order to lose weight felt so terrible. It was like taking away all of the fun, joy, and love.

I know my family wasn't unique in this at all. I grew up in Southern Illinois. This was cultural: you make food to show love and the more you eat, the more you honor the cook.

I know this concept isn't unique to the rural Midwest.

This is exactly what I was teaching my kids as well. Anytime we had something to celebrate, they expected me to make a special dessert. When I thought about celebrating any event, my first thought was what we would eat. I mean, that is pretty much the focus of American holidays—let's get together and overeat! I felt compelled to stick to tradition, making nourishing versions of all the classic foods.

In the course of any given day, eating was one of the only ways that I allowed myself to take time just for me. I think sometimes my snack breaks were more about the breaks than the snacks. I just felt I needed a good reason to stop during the day. Eating food seemed legitimate and necessary, while simply wanting a break felt weak and lazy.

Standing in the kitchen, spoon hovering over my chocolate creation, I could see that this wasn't right. Feeding my body food it didn't need, so I didn't have to go back to work, wasn't kind. Yet, if I removed *all* the treats, all the sweet things—even the nourishing ones—all the foods that I was using for rewards, treats, celebrations, and entertainment, what would be left?

I thought about all the events, big and small, where food played the starring role. If I removed food, there would be a huge hole in my life. I thought about all the pleasure and joy I got from eating food at special events, holidays, or even in the middle of the afternoon by myself. I tried to imagine those times without the joy of food.

Ugh, how depressing.

That was a huge wake-up call for me. I had not realized how much of my daily pleasure and joy was coming from food. That wasn't what I wanted for me or my daughters. I did not want food to be the only source of joy and pleasure in my life or something I couldn't be happy without.

I had made a decision to only eat when physically hungry and stop when physically satisfied. I realized my snacking/ desserts rarely fit the bill. I needed to make a change.

What in the world am I going to do for joy now? Sadly, I realized I wouldn't be able to draw on Aphrodite for this one. I would have to figure out how to find joy in my life outside of food on my own. I scheduled a couple of hours in my calendar later in the week for joy—a time when I could explore what I liked and just do things to bring joy to my life outside of food.

The time came. I closed my computer and stood up from my desk. I made sure the kids were entertained and then stepped into two hours of free time that were dedicated to doing things that would make me feel happy and joyful that didn't involve food.

I remember where I was standing. On the edge of my dining room, facing the entry to the living room. I was in an in-between spot of our home, not really in either room, just waiting for the inspiration to come. I was ready to head off into whatever direction the joy awaited. I felt the cool, smooth wood floor beneath my feet. I breathed deep. *What would bring me joy?* I waited for an answer.

And waited.

And waited some more.

I stood there, between those two rooms, waiting for direction that never came.

Standing there, I realized the cold, hard truth: I had no idea what would bring me joy. I couldn't remember ever asking myself such a question. Honestly, I didn't think I should need to ask it at all. *I should know this! What in the world is wrong with me? This is clearly something any normal human being would know. I'm such a screw-up. I can't even do* joy *right!*

I ended up on the couch, crying over my inability to know what brought me joy. Not very Aphrodite-ish.

Once I was calm, I tried to figure out what in the world went wrong and why. I decided that maybe I wasn't quite ready to do this on my own after all. Maybe Aphrodite could help in some way. So, I grabbed a tissue, dried my eyes and went back to visualizing.

What Would Aphrodite Do to feel joy?

As her image formed in my mind and I prepared to ask her what she did during the day when she wanted to feel joy, I stopped, recognizing my error almost immediately. Watching her in my mind's eye, going about her life, I saw she *already* looked joyful! I had a preconceived idea that I would watch her go *do* things that brought her joy like I was trying to do, but she looked pretty stinkin' joyful right where she was at.

For someone who really, truly, fully, and deeply loved themselves, joy would not be an event that needed to be scheduled on the calendar. She was the goddess of beauty! I imagined just waking up and knowing you were beautiful would have been pretty joyful.

I hadn't really noticed it when I was imagining her before, but as I went through all of my earlier visions, I noticed that she genuinely looked happy in all of them. I know every human gets sad sometimes, but I concluded that for Aphrodite, *joy would be a way of life*. There would have been a measure of joy that she always carried around, because overwhelming self-love would make anyone happy.

Beyond the baseline joy that comes from really loving yourself and loving your body, I became convinced that Aphrodite would have found joy in the everyday things of her life. The mundane. That seemed so much more loving than what I was doing—trudging through hours and days and weeks to get to brief times carved out of my schedule that I actually enjoyed.

I imagined her feeling a desire to do something and then acting on it in the moment. If she wanted to dance, she danced. Wherever.

If she wanted to stop for a moment to really look at the sky, some flowers, or her children, she did.

If she wanted to read, she would read.

If she wanted to go for a walk, she stepped outside and walked.

These would have been simple joys, but multiplied over days and hours and weeks, it would create a joyful life. And, with a life so full of daily joy, there wouldn't be the need to escape face first into a dessert.

Lesson 9: Aphrodite finds joy outside of food.

I, on the other hand, had been operating out of a sense of duty, doing only what I thought I *should* for a long time. I thought that was the right way to do it. I thought that was what made you a good person, a good wife, a good mom—doing what you should. Seeking out joy went against my core wiring. Even though I wanted to find joy in everyday things, I was having major trouble figuring out even one thing to do just for joy that wasn't food-related accomplishment based—I mean, a clean bathtub *did* bring me a measure of joy, but I was looking for something I enjoyed *during*, not just after. *How did it even work? How would she know what she wanted to do at any moment? What if she was busy? Would she drop her responsibilities to follow a whim? Doubtful.*

The only answer I had was vague: she would have to listen to her own heart. She would need to check in with her desires throughout the day. She would have to trust herself. Her heart would be an independent guide that existed in the midst of, but apart from, the other voices of her life.

Well, that sounded nice, but all of that was going to be a real problem when the rubber met the road. I had already established that trusting myself didn't work well, at least not with food. But maybe, just maybe, I could give this a try in some small ways.

I took two baby steps to begin. First, I looked back at my life to see what kinds of things had brought me joy in the past that weren't related to food. Some things were no longer options, like my love of sports. I came face to face with mom life. That changes what options are available during the day.

One of the things that I really enjoyed for a while that I could still do now was reading novels—usually ones with a little romance (Okay, okay. A *lot* of romance). That was something I had only allowed myself to do when I was bedridden, but once I had regained some semblance of productivity, reading ceased. So, I did some research and borrowed a book from the library.

Second, I decided that at least once a day I would just check in with myself to see what I wanted to do in the moment. Maybe I would hear something, maybe I wouldn't. Regardless, I committed to the practice of checking in with myself. I also just generally paid more attention throughout the day to see what I was already enjoying or not enjoying.

I set an intention: do more of what I enjoyed and less of what I didn't—when possible.

I knew I was extending lunch just to avoid returning to work. I decided to let myself read a chapter in my new book during the time when I would typically have been eating a dessert.

The results were astounding. As soon as I had something else that I could do that was exciting to me, leaving the table was easy. Reading a chapter over my lunch break became my "me time" and I thought similarly about my reading as I had about dessert before: *This is just for me. I need a little longer break. A little rest before getting back to work will do me good. This is "me time."* Reading felt good, but in an entirely different way from how eating the food felt good.

This process showed me there were really two kinds of joy: genuine and false. I thought that eating desserts brought me joy. It did make me happy in the moment, but it wasn't real joy. It was a temporary escape from my life. It was a numbing of pain. It felt good for a moment, but I wasn't any better off overall. When it led to emotional overeating, I was actually worse off. I was using food to avoid getting to the real root of problems in my life. It was only a band-aid solution.

Taking a break when I needed it and choosing to spend that time doing something I loved only had upsides as far as I could see. The reading was enjoyable, but I also had a chance to rest my body and be still for a bit. I let my mind and my body come down from the stress that homeschooling often produced. I went back to my day more energized and focused. Plus, I was using food appropriately, which moved me one step closer to living like Aphrodite. This was real joy—with no negative backlash afterward.

I stayed true to my word and checked in with myself once a day, sometimes more. I started paying more and more attention to things I thought brought me joy but were false, and things that really and truly did bring me joy. Not surprisingly, all the things that brought me true, genuine joy had nothing to do with food. They centered on my family, friends, and activities that I enjoyed. I still liked the taste of the food I was eating, but as I spent more time looking for, seeking out, and focusing on ways to enjoy my life outside of food, the draw to go eat desserts began to diminish.

I also felt *way* less desire to cook...like, at all. Cooking had always been my reason to consume those phantom calories that "didn't count." Once the lure of forbidden fruit was removed, I realized that, despite being a good cook, it fell into the category of "don't enjoy." I just didn't love it.

One of the things that got in the way of me learning to find joy in the moment was the voice in my head telling me what I should and shouldn't be doing. I don't know where it came from or how long it had been there, but I would guess since childhood, because the voice often sounded suspiciously like my parents, but also like authority figures in general—pastors, teachers, speakers, authors, and even trusted friends. Most people I talk to have this voice as well, the one that tells you what you *should* be doing.

If I was going to master this joy-from-everyday-life thing, that voice needed to go. It was getting in the way left and right. I remember the day I finally conquered it. It stands out so clearly. I was done with homeschooling the kids and had planned to spend the afternoon on a work project, but I was exhausted. I hadn't slept well the night before and just felt so physically drained and mentally sluggish. I wanted to sit down and read more vampire romance or maybe even watch some TV. Just rest. The problem was that it was the middle of the afternoon and the voice in my head told me I shouldn't rest in the middle of the day. *That's lazy.*

I sighed and looked up. The voice was probably right. I could see cobwebs on the ceiling.

The voice said, *You should clean.*

Standing there in my living room, for the first time, I really registered that voice. I examined it. I took a step back and looked at it for a minute. I had always just obeyed it. I had never really evaluated it objectively. Thanks to my work with Aphrodite, I was becoming increasingly aware of what went on in my head. I examined that thought: *You should clean.* I looked at all the times that voice told me what I *should* or *shouldn't* be doing. I decided I was sick of that voice.

I asked myself, *Says who? Who says I should clean right now?*

The answer? Nobody! Nobody was saying I should clean except me. It wasn't a voice. It was my thoughts. My brain. Me. Maybe it was originally someone else's voice, and maybe now it was a compilation of voices from my childhood, but this was my head and I didn't have to think that if I didn't want to. I certainly didn't have to listen to it or do what it said if I didn't want to.

I mean, seriously, who says we *should* or *shouldn't* do things? Usually it is just us and no one else. Even if it is someone else, why does their opinion matter more than our own? The last time I checked, I was an adult. As an adult, I get to make my own choices about my life. In fact, I am the only one who *can* make those choices, and I am the one who will have to live with them. I decided "shoulds" were no longer for me. I was pretty sure they weren't for Aphrodite either.

So, rather than should-ing (Get it? Sounds like "shitting?" It stinks.) on myself anymore, I turned to my work with the goddess. Instead of asking what I should do, I asked myself, *What Would Aphrodite Do? What would be most loving right now? What would I do if I loved myself?*

I thought about the tasks I was considering doing instead of resting. There wasn't any pressing reason or deadline to get the house clean. It wasn't even that dirty. The work project wasn't time sensitive. This was mostly just my own belief that resting in the middle of the day, even if tired, made you lazy.

I decided, in this case, resting in the middle of the day was the most loving thing I could do for myself.

So I rested.

Even though resting in the middle of the day would never make it onto a top ten list of things that bring me joy, in really did produce joy that day. I leaned into that moment and celebrated my choice to treat my body kindly. I chose to think about my midday rest like Aphrodite would: *This is loving. This is how we care for this body.*

I didn't beat myself up. I didn't call myself names. I owned that I had made a choice based on what I thought was most loving in that moment. It didn't really matter what other people or the voice in my head thought. There was a joy in that I hadn't expected. A joy that is the natural byproduct of showing love to myself in an everyday situation. It made me truly happy to take care of myself in that moment.

Joy can come from many things, but I believe true joy is always rooted in love. It is always a positive and never harmful. It builds up. It helps. It feels great during and after.

As I defined joy more clearly, I realized joy *could* be present at meal times. There was an everyday kind of joy in loving my body and taking care of myself by eating nourishing foods. I love sitting down to a colorful meal. It felt good. No downside.

Even so, I had a longing, a curiosity, a compulsion to cultivate joy in my life—outside of food. I was beginning to see that I didn't need to eat as often as I once did, and I wanted to be able to feel joy at any hour. I never wanted to feel compelled to eat in order to feel joy. I never wanted to have to wait. It was okay if joy was a natural by product of a meal, I just didn't want it to be my motivation for eating.

Joy needed to become a lifestyle.

Chapter 15

Would Aphrodite Exercise?

When it comes to disordered Thoughts, diet edged out exercise by only a hair. The two were very intimately connected for me. With my mealtimes transformed, the next pressing question for me was, would Aphrodite have exercised? My first thought was, NO WAY! Not a chance. Exercise sucked. It was exhausting. It was draining. It was painful. It felt awful emotionally too. It had been my go-to strategy to *change* my body. It was my attempt to make it thinner, trimmer, and more toned. No way would Aphrodite have done that.

There was a time, when I was a child, when I exercised and didn't associate it with my weight. I did it because I liked it or because it was part of a game I enjoyed. In grade school and high school I got a lot of exercise playing sports, and I didn't have any negative associations with that. There was a clear goal: practice, improve, WIN. Winning is fun. I also enjoyed feeling strong, so I lifted weights and did other things that were not directly related to my sports, but would help my athleticism and coordination overall. I even (kind of) enjoyed sprints! I was fast, competitive, and I pushed myself hard. I loved being the first across the finish line even though it burned my thighs so much and I was huffing like a chimney when I was done! It had been over a decade since I was an athlete, and all of that positive association was long gone.

During high school, when I struggled with eating disorders, and on into adulthood, exercise became the way to lose weight. "Burning calories" was my goal. In addition to my sports practice I would run 3 miles before school during the week and 5 miles on weekends. (There is absolutely nothing wrong with running that much, especially if someone is a distance runner. The problem is that I was doing it on a diet of about 800 calories that had little or no nutrition and hating myself every step of the way.) I didn't enjoy the actual run itself, but I always felt better afterwards because I had done something "right."

I burned calories.

I pushed through pain.

I kept my commitments to finish my distance even when it hurt.

I was dedicated.

The very fact that it felt so bad was part of why it felt so good. I hated it, but did it anyway. And that, in my mind, was how it was supposed to be.

Years later, while trying to get stronger after being bed-bound for years, exercise was linked to my disability. It was mostly physical therapy and trying to build enough muscle to not dislocate joints so much, which wasn't awful, but certainly wasn't enjoyable. After I was out of my wheelchair and trying to get stronger, I would exercise every evening because I just couldn't make it happen during the day. I hit the ground running with the kids: Breakfast, homeschool, lunch. I spent a few hours everyday cooking and preparing the special food I needed to stay wheelchair-free. Sometimes I took the kids to park play dates. I filled in the rest of the afternoon hours with working on my business, then making dinner. The first time I would have a free minute was in the evening when the rest of the family was chilling out to watch TV. Instead of joining them on the couch for snuggles, I was on the floor, doing my 2 hours of strength training and pilates. I hated missing time on the couch with the family and felt guilty about it, but I *had* to exercise. It was part of the work that had gotten me out of a wheelchair. Even though it was now mostly regular-looking exercise, it was still physical therapy in many ways.

While I did genuinely need to do my exercises, when I started gaining weight it became more than that. When I started falling back into disordered thinking about my body, those exercises became intertwined with my weight as well. I was genuinely terrified to exercise less than I was, fearing I would end up back in a wheelchair if I lost too much muscle mass. That mindset kept me going. Yet, on any given day, I was tracking my calories consumed and counting on burning those calories in the evening to maintain my current weight. If I skipped it, and didn't burn those calories, then my overall calorie intake would be in the weight gain zone. So, I worked out every night, even when I was so tired I could barely keep my eyes open. On those nights it took even longer to complete my routine, because I went slow and took so many breaks. I would finish and then fall in to bed, dead to the world. It was not pleasant. And, after months of functioning this way, I found myself dealing with adrenal fatigue.

In short, exercise was not something I viewed as positive.

When I thought about all I had learned about Aphrodite, when I thought about all the loving ways she would have thought about her body and all the ways she would have loved it, my version of exercise did not fit. There was absolutely, positively, 100%, no way that Aphrodite exercised the way that I did.

Did that mean she didn't exercise at all?

I tried to imagine Aphrodite, the woman who loves and prizes her body so much, laying around and *never* moving. That didn't seem right either. Never moving would *also* feel bad, just in a different way. Now, as a mom of two littles who had been consistently overdoing and under sleeping for a while, I was pretty sure I could lay on the couch and not move for a solid week or so before I got there, but eventually the inactivity would feel bad.

Clearly, there was a lot to unpack when it came to Aphrodite and exercise.

I found some time for a session with Aphrodite. I sat with my eyes closed to get my mind in Aphrodite's head space. I thought about what she would think and feel about her body: love, acceptance, pride, joy, respect. I tried to really feel those things as well. I reminded myself of all the things I knew about how Aphrodite would have treated this body that she prized and valued. Then I tried to let my mind flow towards movement or lack thereof.

What I saw in my mind was…beautiful.

Carefree.

Happy.

Lovely.

I imagined her stretching her arms up to the sky and down to the ground simply because it feels amazing to do so. I imagined her in a field and choosing to run across the grass just to marvel in the movement of her own limbs. She laughed and smiled and twirled in the sun. I saw her dancing, not as part of a class to burn calories, but because it was fun. I saw her taking walks—not the power walks where the head is down and the arms are furiously pumping, but just a normal walk, eyes raised, enjoying the things she saw. As I watched her, I realized that she certainly moved and actually moved a lot, but not to change her body. She moved *because she wanted to* and because her body wanted to. She moved because it brought her joy.

The phrase "joyful movement" came to my mind as I sat there "watching." It reminded me so much of a child. It reminded me of myself when I was young—swimming for hours and hours or running across the backyard with no thought of calories or how it would affect my body composition. I did it because it felt good. I realized, or perhaps *remembered*, movement *does* feel good. That was a shocking remembrance. Laying around all day doesn't feel great. It makes you stiff, sore, and tired, and there was no way a woman who loved her body would do that.

Aphrodite definitely would have moved.

Even so, I could not equate what I was seeing in my mind with what I thought of as exercise. They barely resembled each other, even though mechanically they were very similar. The difference was in the attitude and the intent. I exercised because I hated my body. She would have moved because she loved hers. The exercise I was doing felt terrible. I was exhausted and sore and damaging my body because, honestly, I was doing too much. She would have moved only in ways that were beneficial and loving to her body. Sometimes she would have worked hard and exerted herself, but I knew she would have listened to her body and stopped when it said to stop.

I ended my session feeling so much lighter. The idea that I could move my body in ways that were beneficial and it could feel good was such a relief! I wanted to cry. Probably did a little. I don't think I really realized how tired I was until I had the thought that it might be over, that I might be allowed to finally rest. That I could stop counting the calories that exercise burned and just *move*.

I decided to try this all out experimentally, knowing that, unlike her body, mine had some "issues" to consider, but I was willing to try it her way.

The next day, I spent some time getting into an Aphrodite mindset: pretending I loved my body and didn't need or want to change it. I spent time checking in to see how I felt and tried to "ask" my body how it wanted to move that day. What sounded good to me was a leisurely stretch and a walk in the sun—so much nicer than my pilates mat in the living room. So, I did that. I tried to keep myself in her mindset as I went, marveling at my limbs, feeling gratitude for the body I had. I walked at a pace that felt good. I noticed what was around me and stopped to smell the roses growing along the sidewalk (Okay, they weren't *literally* roses, but they were flowers and I *did* stop to smell them). I told my body it could stop when it was tired. Despite thinking it would be better to do more, when I began to fatigue, I stopped.

Afterwards I felt...good. I had more energy rather than less. I felt ready to move on with my day, rather than feeling like I need to crash for an hour to recover. I marveled at the difference between this and how I felt when I pushed through exercise while tired.

That night, I snuggled on the couch with my kids for the first time in a long while. We watched TV and I just held them. The next day, I woke feeling less tired than I had in ages.

I continued to check in with my body and tried to choose movement based on what it seemed to be "asking for." Many days, I just did a little light stretching in the evenings, then joined in the cuddles. Some days I did yoga or tai chi or took a walk. Some days I swam. Some days I did my old pilates routine. Some days I didn't "exercise" at all, especially if I had been naturally active during the day from cleaning or taking my kids to the park. With this new mindset, it all felt great in my body.

The only real distress was in my mind. I had a lot of fear around doing less exercise, but it turns out those fears were completely unfounded. The stress of overworking my body was doing more harm than the muscle building had been doing good. By listening to my body, moving when that felt good and not moving when it didn't, I slowly started to feel better over all. My pain was decreasing. I still felt strong, but I was also more alert and aware. I was also more patient with my family and more emotionally stable. I felt happier. The biggest fear, that I would gain weight, was also unfounded. It turns out, being tired can make you feel more hungry. Without the overarching fatigue, I wasn't reaching for snacks as often throughout the day because I already had enough energy.

Perhaps most importantly, this felt sustainable. I had done tons of exercise plans in my life. Tons of programs. Tons of routines that were going to get me the body of my dreams. None of them had done that and I had eventually stopped all of them. Moving my body in loving ways? That was something I could do for a lifetime. This was perhaps the only plan I had ever made which I believed I could do forever. The specific exercises would change from season to season, but I could always choose love at any age or ability level.

I didn't need an exercise plan, I just needed proper motivation, and now I had it: love.

Lesson 10: Aphrodite moves her body in loving ways.

I remember having a conversation with a good friend of mine around this time. Both of us were in a healthy weight range, but both of us also wished our bodies looked different. We were both homeschooling moms with dozens of other responsibilities. As we chatted, I got a chance to verbally process some of my thoughts around exercise, which is often when I have my greatest revelations. (Any other verbal processors out there?) We were chatting about going to the gym and the time commitment of exercise. I said, "We could *totally* have bodies that look like we spend 8 hours in the gym everyday…if we were willing to spend 8 hours in the gym every day! We could hire personal trainers and dietitians. We *totally* could. That is what it would take, though, and I'm just not willing to do that. That isn't what I want for my life."

I was shocked to hear that come out of my own mouth and realize it was true. Yes, I did want to look great, but I wasn't willing to pay that unreasonable price for it. The cost is so much, not just in terms of actual money, but also in time, energy, and focus. I was not willing to have the perfect body at the expense of everything else in my life. I had thought my whole life that I wanted that—to have a perfect body—more than anything. That day, I realized I didn't. Not really.

After that conversation, I spent time thinking about what it was that I really *did* want. It turns out, I wanted to be at peace with myself and my body. I wanted to be happy in my life regardless of the number on the scale. I wanted my life to be about more than my pants size. For the first time, a path toward that type of freedom and possibility felt available to me. I could *direct* my mind to other things. I could create a different life for myself, not centered on how my body looked.

Now, it's true that I also didn't want to be overweight, something that had always terrified me into exercise. As I thought of Aphrodite, I felt really convinced that she would not have been overweight because she would have listened to her body in terms of both eating and movement. She would have been healthy, and that didn't equate to swimsuit model thinness, with 6-pack abs—which had always been my goal. If my goal was to be at peace with my health, normal size body, these lesson from Aphrodite on mealtimes and movement would get me there!

I was still struggling to really believe that my body could give adequate signals to keep me at a healthy weight. It was hard to let go of the rigid exercise plans that I had thought were necessary. It was unnatural for me and different from everything I had learned. Even so, I was becoming more open to the idea that my body could be trusted in this area and that it could tell me when to rest and when to move. I was also beginning to warm up to the audacious notion that I could enjoy movement for movement's sake.

I knew without a shadow of a doubt that movement was loving, and I committed to learning to move for that reason and that reason alone.

Chapter 16

Practicing Aphrodite's Lessons

These sessions with Aphrodite transformed my thoughts on diet and exercise. In the end, I came away with 10 lessons about how a woman who loves her body approaches mealtimes and movement:

1. She is present for her life. Not thinking about food all the time.

2. She sees physical hunger as emotionally neutral. It isn't good or bad, it is just a signal from her body. It is not a cause for panic.

3. She eats when she is physically hungry. Eating for other reasons are not loving.

4. She responds to her body's hunger signals calmly. She will —of course—feed the body she loves. The promise of love and care means that there isn't a rush. Her body will always be fed and cared for.

5. She chooses foods that will nourish her body.

6. Eating is an act of love toward her body. It is done slowly. Food is not a reward or a punishment, but a tangible way of showing the love she feels.

7. She stops eating when she is satisfied, not to lower the calorie count or lose weight, but simply because overeating

is not a loving thing to do to her body. She is always allowed to eat more if there is genuine, physical hunger.

8. She does not feed her body harmful things. She loves her body too much for that.

9. She finds joy outside of food. The things that bring her joy are genuinely good for her and often found in the everyday parts of her life.

10. She moves her body in loving ways. She enjoys movement and honors her body's signals.

These were my starting points. These principles grounded me and centered me in what it looked like to love my body. I regularly went back to the visions of Aphrodite in my mind, because her thoughts and emotions were the lens with which I viewed all of this—always a lens of love.

I spent time before I ate putting myself in her head space.

I worked to remember the lessons.

I switched to her thoughts about exercise before choosing what to do for the day.

It was a process and a journey. You may have breezed through reading these chapters, but this was not quick for me—I'm talking daily work month after month. I was regularly confronted with old mindsets, beliefs, and fears. They popped up all throughout the day. Anytime I did not direct my brain to think like Aphrodite, I still thought like me. I persisted. I kept working to love my body like Aphrodite and make *that* the new habit. I had experienced the power of telling my brain what to think and seeing real emotional change.

Every meal I was able to imitate Aphrodite and eat from a place of love was a victory. Every time I found joy outside of food, I soared. Every time I exercised and felt better rather than worse, I marveled at the simplicity of it all: Love your body.

Aphrodite was my hero.

By eating this way, I started to feel better overall.

My mood and energy were more stable from eating more consistently, and I didn't feel ravenous when I sat down to eat because I was answering my hunger sooner.

I was also eating more fat and nourishing foods that helped me feel more satisfied with less.

Despite eating less food—because my food choices were more concentrated—I wasn't missing the higher quantity of food as much as I predicted I would. In fact, all the chewing and being totally present with each bite sometimes got really tedious! Eating less sometimes felt like a relief.

Eating only when hungry meant more time in my regular life. Now that I was seeking out (and finding) more things that brought me joy, that was becoming a good thing.

I had more energy to give to Chris and Zoe and Nadia, as I gave less to unnecessary workouts.

I was still mimicking Aphrodite's love for her body…

…but loving my life?

That was becoming more real every day.

Part 3: Ending The War

Chapter 17

Battle Lines

Freedom around mealtimes and movement was something I had rarely allowed myself to hope for during the early weeks and months of my WWAD method. Yet now, thanks to Aphrodite, freedom was mine. I was learning to eat and move like I loved myself. Everyday I practiced. Everyday I got better. Everyday it became more natural to nourish my body and not harm it, caring for it like it was my most prized possession. I thought differently about food, I felt differently when I was around it, and I was speaking about it in different ways—more loving ways. I felt hope for the first time in a long time that I might be able to end the cycle of disordered eating. If I could keep this up, my daughters might never go through what I went through. They might never deal with the obsession around food and exercise. They might never feel the need to go on a diet. They might have a mom who was a solid example of what it looked like to have a healthy relationship with food.

If I had stopped right there, my life would have been forever changed for the better, but I didn't *want* to stop there. The more time I spent hanging out with Aphrodite, the more areas I discovered that were in desperate need of her loving touch. There were so many ways that I wasn't loving myself or my body that had nothing to do with food or exercise. I decided to see how deep this rabbit hole went. But, before I could move onto the next area of my life, I needed to address a recently discovered roadblock in my progress towards fully adopting all of the earlier lessons: I was struggling to hear from my body throughout the day.

Some aspects of Aphrodite's lessons could be done ahead of time. For example, I spent time deciding in advance what I wanted to think in all the situations that I could anticipate around mealtimes and exercise—getting hungry, preparing food, sitting down to eat, being satisfied while food remained on my plate, and thoughts about movement—then I simply repeated those thoughts at the proper cue. I spent time appraising various foods when I wasn't actually eating to determine if I thought they were a loving option for my body. I decided not to eat certain ones, like refined sugar, because they would harm my body. I did this work during times of emotional clarity, typically right after a session with Aphrodite. In these cases, loving myself simply meant honoring the decisions I had already made.

The rest of the work centered on body awareness—noticing hunger signals, recognizing when I was satisfied, and distinguishing physical hunger from an emotional desire for food. That awareness required listening to my body *in the moment*. I couldn't do it once and then reuse the information. It was daily, hourly, minute by minute. I knew it was a vital, key skill for ultimate success in this process. Sadly, I sucked pretty badly at it.

I was very good at the opposite: being unaware of my body. In fact, I had spent most of my life training myself to ignore my body's signals. As a young child, my parents told me to finish everything on my plate, even if I was full. As a grade schooler, my gymnastics instructor said I was too thin and lacked the muscle needed for power tumbling, so my mom would spoon

121

feed me chocolate pudding while I lay on the couch, even though I didn't want it and wasn't hungry. As an athlete, I learned to push through fatigue, pain, and even injury for the sake of winning. As a teenager, I learned to ignore hunger in order to lose weight. As an adult, I learned to eat well past fullness when it was a special occasion. As a mom I learned to ignore fatigue in order to care for my kids. As a wife, I learned to ignore my wants in order to care for our home. During my disability, I learned to ignore physical pain to get through the day.

Until my work with Aphrodite, I thought this was just how it was done. Ignore. Push through. Dig Deep. Buckle Down. Do the "right" thing.

I was *very* good at this. During the worst of my health trials, my physical therapist often noted how high my pain tolerance was during treatment. I saw this as a badge of honor. Honestly, I still do in some ways. I don't believe I actually experienced the pain less severely than others—believe me when I say that many of my treatments were horrifically painful. I was just good at forcing myself to not respond to it. I wouldn't allow myself to cry out or make more than the smallest noises, even though I wanted to scream. I worked very hard to ignore the pain and go somewhere else in my mind. I pretended it wasn't happening. At home after these treatments, I would sleep or get lost in books or TV to check-out mentally when the pain became too much to ignore—and that was most of the time.

In each of these cases, ignoring my body's signals seemed like the right thing to do. Faced with extremely high levels of pain and no end in sight, I was just trying to find a way to survive and get through the day. I didn't know of any other way to do it. Honestly, I am not sure I would have survived being fully present with all the physical and emotional pain of my condition, having no knowledge (at that time) of how to process something so intense.

Regardless of the validity of my reasons, every choice has consequences and now I was facing mine. My previous decisions to practice ignoring my body were hindering me now. I needed to be able to do the opposite. I needed to really listen to my body and I had no idea how to do that. I had no personal experience with that kind of awareness. I didn't even know where to start.

While all of that is true, I also knew it was *more* than a lack of knowledge, skill, or practice that was thwarting my efforts. This went beyond a learned behavior or habit. There was a barrier between me and the signals from my body. I knew my body was sending them, and I knew I needed to hear them, but they weren't being received.

When I was actively embodying Aphrodite and her love, I felt like I could listen and hear. I could distinguish between hunger and emotion. I could access her amazing wisdom and her thoughts, and that had allowed me to make some really significant change in my life. Now I needed to marry the exceptional moments with my everyday life. I couldn't go sit on the sofa with Aphrodite every time I needed to hear from my body. One, it was time consuming. Two, I was pretty sure that isn't how it is supposed to work. It felt like something else was missing. I needed to figure out what it was.

I'm generally not a procrastinator. If you're familiar with Strengths Finder, my top strength is Achiever, which means I like getting things done. The more things I check off my to do list each day, the happier I am. I don't put things off, I don't let things pile up. Yet I had been putting *this* off for other more urgent things. *This* stayed on the back burner of my mind for weeks and didn't even make it onto the to do list. I found myself *very* busy organizing closets, deep cleaning the fridge, and organizing long-forgotten files on my computer.

Eventually, I found myself on hands and knees, elbow deep in cleaning products, sporting yellow rubber gloves while meticulously shining the back of the toilet. This was getting out of hand...and I was running out of things to clean. In a moment of clarity and brutal honesty, kneeling before my porcelain throne, I admitted the truth to myself: I didn't *want* to figure it out because I didn't *want* to listen to my body. I didn't want to connect with it or tune into it's signals.

It's the enemy. It's the source of all our pain. It's the cause of all our problems. It's broken. It's defective. It's worthless. It always ruins everything. It doesn't deserve to be heard.

The harsh truth was that my body and I were not on the same team. We were on opposing sides of a war. Me vs. My Body. We were divided by a wide gulf that was filled with all the anger, shame, guilt, and hatred I felt towards my body.

So, yeah, there *was* a barrier that was keeping me from hearing from my body—me. My body had been a jerk, and I was giving it the silent treatment. I was keeping it at arm's length, holding myself apart from it. At times we had been in outright conflict, but now it was the cold war.

If I ever wanted to get to a place where I could act in loving ways toward my body all of the time, even just to fake it for my girls, I would have to end the silent treatment and re-open the lines of communication. I would have to pay attention to physical signals, be aware of my body, and respond appropriately. I would have to actually *feel* what was happening in my body.

I knew that needed to happen. Yet, I was actively resisting moving forward with any sort of reconciliation. There was so much history there. So much pain. There were decades of negative emotions buried in the no-man's-land between me and my body. I didn't want to unearth them. I knew it would be painful to do so and I had this fear that, should I step into the proverbial war zone and raise the white flag, I would be overwhelmed by all the consequences of surrender. I was afraid I would end up back in a state of deep depression; pulled under, buried alive, and unable to find my way back to anything resembling normal life.

I couldn't go there. I had responsibilities. I had a family. It was mission critical that I didn't break.

It seemed easier, safer, to leave it buried.

As much as I wanted to do just that, I couldn't completely bypass my past and jump straight to love. To get there I would first have to deal with the gulf. Addressing the buried emotions might move me to a place where I wouldn't have to actively *choose* loving my body over hate or anger. *Could love become my* default *setting?*

I didn't think Aphrodite would ever have been in a place where she was angry with her body, so I couldn't imitate her here. I would have to do this work as *me,* but I would take her along with me. I would keep her as my guide, my North Star to remind me where I was going. She would be a reference point for loving myself along this new and terrifying journey.

I decided that, in order to know how to let go of the anger and hatred I felt, I needed to know how they got there in the first place. Knowing the reason I was angry with my body might give me a clue how to finally let it go.

How *did* I get to this place where I saw my body as an enemy?

Chapter 18

The Schism

I have heard it said that every "body" has its own story. I thought over my body's story, beginning in early childhood. I don't have a lot of distinct memories from my early years, just some disjointed images. There were a variety of memories of playing with my sister, but wasn't sure when they took place. One of the first really clear ones I had that related to my body was of a favorite outfit that I had when I was 4 or 5. It was a black and white outfit with a cat on it. The shorts had an attached skirt. I wore it every day that it was clean, often asking my mom to do extra laundry so it *would* be clean. I loved spinning in circles and watching the skirt twirl. I also remember looking at my body dressed in it and having zero judgement about the body that was wearing it. I would look at the little body in the mirror, dressed in her favorite outfit, and just feel *happy*. I *loved* the outfit. While I don't remember feeling any specific love for my body, I didn't feel anything negative either. I think my body was just *my body*.

I remember seeing skinned knees and bruised shins. I know I would have seen my hands and arms often, anytime I reached for something. I would have seen my face in the mirror when I brushed my teeth each day. No judgements. They were simply *my* legs, *my* shins, *my* hands, *my* face, and *my* teeth. They weren't good or bad legs, thin or fat legs, they were just *mine*. I hadn't yet learned to judge the body I had.

As a child I was able to hear my body's signals. I knew when I was hungry and when I was full. I remember lots of arguments with my parents about how much food I *should* be eating. I remember being scolded for not liking the taste of what was served. Despite what they said, I knew when I had had enough without having to make a special appointment to check in with my hunger. I knew what I liked and what I didn't. Only the threat of punishment would compel me to eat foods I didn't enjoy or wasn't hungry for, and sometimes even then I wouldn't. I would sit at the table for hours, crying and refusing to eat the meatloaf that was served—I still don't enjoy beef to this day.

I connected with that child and followed her in my mind's eye as she aged. I saw her playing sports and reveling in how fast she was. I saw her sincere appreciation for what her body could do. I saw an unwavering confidence in her own abilities. I saw her dreams for the future. She had no doubt that she could do whatever she set her mind to. Her body was the vehicle she used and I saw her complete trust in its capabilities.

Then I saw other little snapshots along the way—a comment here or there about the chubby cheeks she had when she was young. I remembered statements that had been made that caused her to begin to label the body she had—short, small, muscular, boyish. I saw how those comments could have contributed to a poor body image later on, but they hadn't tipped the scale. All the way through the end of 6th grade, the thoughts about her body were more positive than negative. She *liked* the body she had. It was great and it served her well.

Then, I saw the day it all changed.

I was in 7th grade at a casual event in the school cafeteria. These were occasionally provided by the school after basketball games for the Jr. High and High School students to hang out. They played music and it was similar to an informal dance. Part way through this particular evening, I found myself parched from dancing and talking, so I walked over to get a drink from the snack table. As I picked up the cold can of soda, an older, high school boy approached me and asked if I wanted to go on a drive with him. I knew who he was, though he had never spoken to me before. He was an athlete, attractive, and popular. I said yes, with the agreement that we would be back before my mom came to pick me up since I wasn't technically supposed to leave.

As we drove away, I felt so special to be picked by someone so much older than me. It felt like it set me apart from my peers. I had dated lots of boys, beginning in pre-school, and thought he might want to be my boyfriend—to me, that meant shyly asking me to be his girlfriend and (maybe) awkwardly holding hands in the dark at some point; eventually some kissing as well.

I quickly learned that that was not what he had in mind. He drove all of 5 blocks, parked the car in an alley, removed his seat belt, started kissing me, and then slipped his hand up my shirt. I was 13.

I froze. It felt like my brain and all my insides were paralyzed. I was unable to sort through the confusion in my head to form a coherent thought, let alone find my voice to say no to his advances. I did not want him to touch me the way he was, *but I had no idea what I was supposed to do about it.*

Based on what I could observe as a kid, my parents seemed to handle conflict in one of two ways: yelling or giving the silent treatment. Neither of those seemed to apply there, parked in the alley, and I wasn't really sure what other options there

128

were. I did not want him to touch me that way, but I also didn't want to make him angry. I didn't want to be mean or yell at him because I wasn't sure if he had actually done anything wrong. I didn't want to do anything that might make him not like me anymore, because at the time, him liking me felt really important. I tried to signal with my body that I didn't want to be touched that way, trying to block his roaming hands with my own. I shyly deflected further, more major advances, but it had gone far enough. He drove me back to the dance, clearly super happy with the progress he had made and talking about the next time we could hang out.

I felt dirty.

I grew up attending church and based on the teachings I had heard, I believed I had just sinned in a major, irreversible, life-altering way. I could ask for forgiveness and God would give it, but I was no longer pure. My body was now tainted. I hadn't asked for that touch, but did that matter? Did it matter that I hadn't wanted it? I didn't know. I reasoned it might be my fault, because I went in the first place and should have known better. I went and I didn't make him stop. I had tried to say no with my body language, and may have even said no with my words, but my "no" hadn't been heard. I hadn't made it clear. He hadn't gotten the message, so clearly, I didn't do it "right." *This was my fault.*

Honestly, there is probably some truth to that. If my current self was in that car, you better believe he would have heard my, "No," and that, "No" would have been enforced. But in 7th grade, I had never heard of a boundary. I had certainly never been taught how to properly set one or how to firmly enforce it if it wasn't respected. I didn't know how to say no and be heard. All I knew was that you weren't supposed to have sex before you were married. Holding hands with my 5th grade boyfriend seemed fine, but I had no clue where this 7th grade situation fell.

That day in the car happened so long ago. I don't remember what I was wearing or the type of car he drove. I don't remember the exact words that were said or how long we were gone. I do know without a shadow of a doubt that I did not say, "Yes," to being touched that way. I wasn't consulted, and that means it wasn't okay. Unfortunately, the 7th grade version of me didn't know that consent was required in these situations. I wish she had. Perhaps it would have saved her from what came next.

I felt such deep, unrelenting shame after that day, but didn't know what to do with it. Based on what I had heard other girls saying, I was pretty sure I shouldn't even feel shame at all. That type of situation was, apparently, normal for anyone who was dating. Others were doing much more sexually than what had happened to me in the car, yet they seemed genuinely happy about it. They didn't appear to feel ashamed at all. It seemed like I wasn't *supposed* to feel this way. And yet, I did.

I didn't have anyone in my life who I could go to with this situation. There was no one with whom I felt safe talking openly. When I thought about all the people I knew, I feared being judged, shamed further, or made fun of if I tried to express my confusion. So, I hid it. I didn't tell anyone about what happened, and in that darkness, the shame grew and grew.

That initial shame was compounded with similar incidents repeated throughout the rest of my junior high and high school years. I kept finding myself in similar situations and not wanting to be there—many of which were of my own making, which was confusing to me. I didn't know how to say no in the car that day in 7th grade, and I never learned. I felt like someone was in the wrong each time, but I never really knew if it was me or if it was someone else. I assumed it was me. I am grateful that I was never raped, but there were numerous situations that were very far from consensual, and left me feeling wounded, confused, and used.

Each time that my body was touched and used in a way that I didn't want, but felt powerless to stop, the shame grew. For a while, I was able to continue on normally even with the shame growing inside me. I played sports and went to school. I hung out with friends and watched movies. I went to work and dated. I had some dating experiences and kisses that *were* consensual, experiences that at the time I would have labeled as "normal." However, my adult self can see how every single interaction with the opposite sex was influenced by what I thought was expected and unavoidable. I wanted to fit in. The use of my body seemed like the cost to buy into the "in" crowd. If you wanted to have a boyfriend and keep him, this is what was necessary.

Every experience was accompanied by guilt and shame.

Over the course of 7th and 8th grade, I started to think that maybe there was something wrong with me. I felt sad more and more. I noticed many of my smiles felt fake.

Time passed. The more I thought about it, the more I became convinced it was true. There was *definitely* something wrong with me. I looked around at all my classmates who seemed to really know who they were and had genuine friendships. I felt like I was pretending all the time. I was different than the others somehow. I felt like I couldn't let people see who I really was. I couldn't share how messed up I felt inside. I needed to hide the truth. I needed to pretend to be better than I actually was.

Then, at one point, a thought crept in that maybe I didn't *deserve* any better. Maybe being used by the opposite sex for my body was as good as it was going to get for me. Maybe that was the price someone like me had to pay for companionship. I was less-than, broken, impure, sinful, unworthy. Someone like that didn't deserve good things.

I began to truly believe these dark thoughts about myself and eventually grew to not only dislike myself, but to loathe myself. The shame was ever-present and crushing me with it's weight. I was hurting so deeply and looking for a way to feel better.

Then, conveniently, one presented itself.

When I was 15, the boy from the car (who had since become my boyfriend) picked me up. We were supposed to go to lunch. Instead, he headed in the opposite direction. When I asked where he was going, he said we were going back to his place to work off some calories. Then he winked at me. I knew he meant he was expecting me to pleasure him sexually. I had been able to avoid being pressured into intercourse so far and hoped I could avoid it that day as well, but I knew I would have to do something I didn't want to do before we could go to lunch or do whatever else we were going to do that day.

While on the short drive to his place, I prepared myself for what was going to happen. I had been learning to disconnect my full awareness to my body. I would retreat to a place in my mind where I could dull the experience and protect myself from the inevitable onslaught of shame. Up until that day, I had only separated myself for a short while, just long enough to get through those times.

As I rode in the car anticipating his advances and disconnecting from my body, my brain made some links between food, eating, my body, and sexual shame. It latched onto an opportunity for relief. I decided that the real enemy here was *my body*.

It's the problem. It's the enemy. It's the source of all the pain. This is where the shame happened. This is where we're dirty. If boys weren't attracted to this body, they wouldn't have touched it in those ways. It is my body's *fault.*

Yes. That was it.

It felt really good to have something to blame other than *me*.

A house divided cannot stand and I was ready to crumble. So, I separated in a more lasting way. I became two. There was *me* and there was *my body*. I sacrificed one to save the other and directed all the shame, guilt, and hatred at this vessel that I saw as the source of all my pain. After that day, the schism was permanent.

And I acted precisely the way a person acts who hates their body.

I starved it, denying it the pleasure of food.

I punished it with long hours of exercise, regardless of pain or fatigue.

I thought hateful thoughts about it.

I insulted it.

I was constantly criticizing it.

I kept losing weight, even when I was overly thin and my body was eating its own muscle tissue.

I knew that it wasn't really about the weight, but once I started, I couldn't seem to stop. So I kept going for years. I was obsessed with being thin, yes. I definitely also suffered from dysmorphia, obsessing about my body's flaws and struggling to have an objective sense of its true proportions. Even so, I really think all of that was secondary. The real issue was that I had separated from my body and felt such a strong hatred for

133

it. The starvation and over-exercising of my eating disorder was a way I could punish my body.

Hurting it seemed appropriate to me.

Seeing it skeletal and lacking vitality seemed right.

It felt like penance.

Anyone who has had an eating disorder will likely agree that it's difficult to explain the hows and whys in clear-cut ways. There were likely many factors that led to my disordered eating and this was just one part of it. Yet, looking back, I believe that the catalyst for launching into disordered eating was my need for a scapegoat. I needed someone, or something, to blame for the pain I was in because I didn't know what to do with it. This was when I started feeling—and identifying myself as—separate from my body, and I never came back from it. Even when I was married, eating normally, and not outwardly hurting my body, I still thought of *me* as separate from *my body*.

Just because I'm sharing this part of my story, please know that I am by no means saying every bit of my time from 7th grade to Senior year was horrible. I have loads of fun, beautiful memories as well. But even in the best of times, I always carried around this shame and growing sense of loathing toward my body. I always felt different, other, shameful, less-than, and often mildly depressed without really knowing why. My guess is that many of you reading this can relate. Maybe you understand what it is like to go about your day and really enjoy the people you are talking to and really feel thankful for things, while *also* feeling shame or self loathing. It is totally possible. From that one day in 7th grade on, that was my life.

Then came all of the years of chronic health issues in my mid-twenties. The diagnosis of Ehlers Danlos Syndrome was not the "straw that broke the camel's back" in any way. The camel's back was already good and broken. I already believed my body was the enemy. I already saw it as a problem. I already thought of it as separate. The diagnosis and ongoing health issues were simply "one more thing." One more bit of evidence to throw on the pile of reasons I hated my body.

I can also see how the ongoing health issues contributed to a desire to think of myself as separate from my body. My husband would often joke about me being issued a defective model (referring to my body) and suggest that we simply send it back and try to get a replacement. I wholeheartedly agreed! It was lighthearted and fun to think of it that way—simply being given a defective model. To think of *myself* as broken and defective would have been heart-wrenching, but believing it was just *my body* that was broken gave me a target for my anger and frustration over my situation, and I had a lot of it.

Ending this war with my body would involve dealing with all that anger, all that shame, all that loathing. It would involve a laying down of arms, a ceasefire in this battle that had been raging inside me since I was 13. Above all, it would involve healing the rift between my two halves and finding a way to put them back together.

Perhaps, *then* I would be able to hear the signals.

I needed to find a way to be whole again.

Chapter 19

Cease Fire

I was raised to believe that, when we die, our body decomposes and our soul goes to heaven. Did you know there are some people who believe we actually *keep* our current bodies after we die? I remember the day that someone told me they believed that and all the reasons why. I was decidedly *not* on board with this line of reasoning, regardless of promises of "glorified" versions. I didn't even want to *hear* about such things. At the time, deeply entrenched in my own body hatred, I couldn't imagine anything more horrible. When I was in terrible levels of pain or in the extreme depths of self-loathing because of my weight, I would console myself with one singular thought: *one day, I will be free of this vessel. Hallelujah, amen!* The idea that I might be stuck with it for all of eternity was an unbearable thought.

I don't want this body. It's defective. I don't like it.

These thoughts popped up any time I got ready to approach the next step of my journey. Every time I thought more about how to make peace with my body, I became livid. I wanted to scream at someone—everyone—and tell them: *My body doesn't deserve absolution. It failed me! It's the problem! It can't be trusted! This is a bad idea! Don't do it!*

Dealing with that type of anger was the first hurdle. I could not put my halves back together while I was still being constantly torn apart by rage. It was one of the main barriers to wholeness. I could not feel love for my body while being spitting mad. I would first have to let go of all the anger, all the animosity, all the blame. I would have to, essentially, forgive my body. Only then would there be room for love, acceptance, and peace.

But how?

I began by just asking myself, "*Why* am I angry?" I wrote it all out.

My body is broken. It's defective. It's the reason I couldn't hold my newborn. It's the reason I can't have more kids. It's the reason I missed whole years of my daughters' childhood. It's the reason I can't do activities I love. It isn't fair that I have this condition. My body is gross. It's fat. It's ugly. It's not shaped right. It makes buying clothes hard. It's too short. It's weak. It's keeping me from living the life I want to live. It failed me. It's defective.

The tirade went on and on. Apparently, I had a lot of reasons I was angry at my body.

As I looked at the list, I could see that most of what I had written came down to one key theme: the belief that my body had failed me. I had a clear expectation of what my body was *supposed* to be like—thin and healthy—and it wasn't. I had piles and piles of evidence that *proved* my body's failure. Yet, every time I thought about that evidence, it got me nowhere. I only felt terrible—angry, sad, frustrated, disappointed. Thinking about how my body failed me clearly wasn't helping me, even if it *was* true. I needed a new way of thinking about my body. A shift in perspective. A new story to tell. A reframe. I couldn't come up with one right away, but I kept my eyes up and my ears open.

A few weeks after making my list, a friend of mine was talking about an unconventional weight loss book she had just read and thought I might like. I drove to the library, checked it out, and started reading. As I turned page after page, I was given more and more evidence that our bodies do what they do— whether gaining weight or losing it—based on the signals *we* send it, signals that come from our thoughts and emotions. The author talked about the power of visualization, primal reactions, and our gut brain. It was very thought provoking. It also made me start questioning the blame I felt towards my body.

Maybe I had played more of a role in all of this than I thought. Maybe my body was just responding to what I "told" it subconsciously. *Could that be true? Was it possible that my body had never been working against me?* Maybe it was *trying* to be thin and all my yo-yo dieting had messed it up.

If my body were personified, I guessed it didn't *want* to be in pain any more than I wanted to be experiencing it. It wouldn't *choose* to be overweight or malfunctioning. Maybe it was *trying* to get better but couldn't for some reason. That seemed reasonable. When I thought that way, rather than feeling anger, I felt compassion. I started to see my body as a fellow sufferer, rather than the source of my pain.

We were in this together.

We were both hurting.

My anger at my body was completely misplaced.

As I turned the final page and closed the book, I didn't immediately rise. I sat on my couch, book in hand, and tried to summarize all the concepts I had just taken in. I came up with this: "My body is on my side."

If I could truly believe that my body and I were on the same side, then it would be ridiculous to fight with it. If I could convince myself that we were *truly* in this together, then I could end the war. With one sentence, one thought, the fighting could stop. I gripped the book edges tighter while I considered it. I thought about how things had been going and how tired I was. I decided I was up for some peace. I stood up, put the book in the pile to go back to the library, and stepped into my new reality. Just like that.

I committed to believing this new thing about my body. It didn't happen instantly, but over and over and over again, I repeated, *My body is on my side.*

I reminded myself of it anytime my brain started to tell a story about how it had failed me. Anytime I thought about my body, I tried to do so with a sense of compassion.

I looked for evidence that this new thought could be true. I thought about the things I knew about the human body and all the intricacies of its functions.

I visualized the little cells in my body working hard all day long to get better, but simply having an overwhelming amount of backlogged work to do.

My body is on my side.

I worked on this one sentence until I began to truly believe it.

The day that, *My body is on my side*, felt more true than, *My body has failed me*, I took a deep breath and let the anger go.

That may sound cliche, to just "let it go," but it is truly the best way I can describe what happened. I had been perpetuating and renewing the emotion of anger by thinking about how my body had failed me. I continually fueled it with my list of evidence that I would run through in my mind anytime I started to think about my health condition or my body size.

Once I dismantled and replaced that thought, the anger wasn't anchored to anything solid anymore. There was no longer anywhere to direct the anger, and I found it was gradually fading as my compassion for my body solidified. The only way to make that ethereal presence of remembered anger solid again would be to drum up something to fuel it. I knew I *could* do that, and a part of me wanted to. The anger was familiar and it felt really justified in light of everything I had been through, but I didn't actually *want* it anymore even if it made sense to some part of me. So, I simply let it fade away.

I made a decision that day to never take up arms against my body again, no matter what happened. I wouldn't blame it. I wouldn't see it as an enemy. I would choose to always see us as comrades, fighting for a common goal of health and wellbeing. As the last echoes of anger faded, peace entered and took its place.

It was time to start working together.

Chapter 20

Peace Talks

When I was 10, my friend Stacy and I got best friend necklaces —one where a heart is split into two pieces and each person wears half of it. It was so fun to see each other and put the halves back together to make a whole heart. If only putting my own halves back together were that easy.

The anger towards my body was just an echo, but I still thought of it as separate from me. To rediscover the childhood sense of wholeness and be able to listen to its signals, I would have to remove the division entirely. I had to reunite the halves.

I wanted to get to the place where I saw my body and myself as one, the way I had when I was young, but that felt like a *huge* leap after ignoring it so completely for so long. Saying, "My body and I are one," triggered a veritable flurry of negative emotions. I realized that was the final destination, but I needed a more accessible first step.

Chris and I didn't jump straight from strangers to a married couple. First, we had to meet and get to know each other. Then, there was dating and engagement. *Then,* we became one flesh.

None of that would have happened if I had never seen him, and acknowledged his existence. Pretty basic, but super necessary.

My body and I needed to start at the beginning. I needed to stop ignoring it and pretending it wasn't there. I needed to acknowledge that my body existed.

I have a body.

When I said that sentence to myself, I experienced something I hadn't felt around my body in a long time: quiet. Typically, when I thought about my body, I was super negative. This one thought was so basic, so factual, so…neutral.

I *did* have a body. I always had. *Of course.* It had mass. It had weight. It was a specific height. It had a certain color hair and eyes and skin tone. I didn't have to work to believe this. I could look in the mirror and see it. I could feel the curves and edges. It made so much sense to me once I thought about it.

I have a body.

The profound part of this wasn't the sentence itself, but how it *felt* when I said it. Or, more specifically, how it *didn't* feel. It didn't hurt to think this.

Throughout recent years, every time I thought about my body, I was thinking awful, hateful things about it. I judged every flaw. I said terrible things. I knew that judgement, anger, and shame would always come after any acknowledgement of my body, so it was less painful to just not think about it at all. If I never thought about my body, I didn't have to think about the fact that it was fat and ugly.

I blocked everything out. I avoided looking at myself in mirrors. I put off clothes shopping when I could. I avoided the scale. I generally tried my best to not think about it at all.

But *this*. This new way of thinking about my body didn't hurt.

I began actively releasing all the labels I had attached to my body—good, bad, fat, thin, broken, whole, pure, dirty—and just focused on the fact that I had one. I worked to practice thinking of my body simply as *mine*.

I have a body.

This is my body.

It was such a relief! All my judgments had been so heavy and had been weighing me down. Thinking of my body without labels relieved me of a huge burden that I hadn't realized I was carrying. There was so much freedom in choosing not to judge the body I had, but simply acknowledging I had one.

I have a body.

This simple thought was allowing me to get some genuine traction. Without the judgment, I found I *could* think about my body. I could really acknowledge its existence in my own mind without being instantly repelled. Now we were getting somewhere.

I have a body.

Chapter 21

Reconciliation

Once I settled into the thought of *I have a body*, the next thought flowed out on it's own: *And that body has needs.* That made clear, logical, unemotional sense. If I had a physical body, that physical body had needs.

Without all the judgments that typically came when I thought of my body, I actually felt ready to start listening to the body I had. I just wasn't quite sure how it worked on a practical level.

One evening, after the kids were in bed, I propped up a couple pillows and settled onto my bed with a notebook and pen. I decided I would just do some brainstorming and see what came up. I wrote things like, *How do people listen to their bodies? How can I listen to my body? How will I know what it needs? How can I tune into its signals?*

I looked at my paper and the lightbulb went off.

Ah. I see.

My eyes zeroed in on the language I was using. I was still saying, "My body." I referred to my body as an "it." Despite acknowledging my body, I still thought of it as a thing that existed apart from me. Well, it kind of does though, right?

I knew I was more than just flesh, bone, skin, and blood. I could cut off an arm and still be me, so I wasn't just my body. At the same time, I had seen how interrelated all the parts of me were. When I dislocated a joint in my body the pain affected my ability to think clearly, and I had experienced brain damage from repeated concussions that caused genuine personality changes.

I spent the better part of a week just pondering all of this and much more, safely following numerous theological, physiological, and esoteric rabbit trails in my mind before I caught on to the real issue. This was not a matter of me figuring out the mysterious connection between the material and immaterial parts of me. I didn't need to figure out the secrets of the universe. God may have the ability to separate out the various parts of a human, but I, Lorrie Gray, do not. While I am alive, living as a human on planet earth, all my parts, no matter how you theoretically divide them, are functioning together as the single entity that is *me*. They are intimately intertwined, and what happens to one part affects the others. What I do to my physical body affects my mind and emotions. What I think and feel affects my body. It is an ongoing loop, for better or worse.

As a human being, the things that happened in my physical body were part of my experience. They were a part of being human. They were a part of life—my life. And I was missing them! I was disconnecting myself from the human experience of having a body, trying to divide myself up into different parts. Keeping them separate is not truly possible. I have only ever been one.

I recognized that, grammatically, there is absolutely nothing wrong with saying "my body" or at times using the pronoun "it." I could see that very often that would be the correct language to use. The shift for me was the intent behind those words and the reason I used them.

I needed to start viewing myself as a whole person. I had to reintegrate my physical body into my own understanding of myself. So, I worked to change that language anytime it made sense to. I chose to say, "I am" rather than, "My body is," to keep driving this point home for myself.

I said, "I am in pain," not, "my body is in pain."

I said, "I am hungry," not "my body is hungry."

I said, "I am tired," not "my body is tired."

These were all physical sensations that were originating in my physical body, but I was experiencing them as a whole person and would need to respond to them as a whole person. There was no way to *only* respond to a need physically. I was always experiencing it in my soul as well. I was thinking thoughts and having emotions. I had seen how hunger, which was physical and happening in my body, had produced panic before I changed my thoughts about it. I had never been able to *just* feel hunger, eat, and stop eating when full without having thoughts about the hunger and the eating. I couldn't eat without any emotions whatsoever.

What I had naturally felt in response to these sensations had always been so negative that I had tried to shove down and resist what I was experiencing.

Now, there was no anger, because I knew my body was on my side. There was no judgement, because I chose to only think of the fact that I had a body without attaching labels to it. My body and I were one, and together there were needs that had to be met. Needs that originated in a variety of places but that would be met by the whole person that is *me*.

This is how I would become whole. I would recognize and acknowledge that I was experiencing everything as a whole person. I would meet my physical needs as a whole person, experiencing thoughts and emotions and including them in my process. I would pay attention to the interaction of all parts. I wouldn't let some in and ignore the rest. I would let it all in.

I have a body.

This is my body.

This is the only body I have.

It has needs.

I *am going to take care of it.*

I began to see each lesson Aphrodite had taught me in a new light. I went back and revisited them all from this new perspective. The lessons were the same, but there was a greater depth to *why* I was choosing to move in loving ways, eat nourishing foods, and avoid things that were harmful: my body and I were one. We had always been one. I had never been able to isolate harm to my physical body. I also could not isolate love.

Feeling genuinely whole came with time, but the decision to respond to each need as a whole person without trying to divide up my experience unlocked my ability to start paying attention. The more I acknowledged myself, the more I began to truly feel like a whole person.

It made me aware of myself on a whole new level. I saw more clearly how my emotions affected my experience. I saw how I could change attitudes. I began seeing the connections, the interactions, the overlaps. I was intricate and complex. It was kind of beautiful once I thought of it. A little messy at times, but beautiful.

For the first time, this was not me imitating Aphrodite. I wasn't pretending to be a whole person.

I had done this work.

Aphrodite had been my inspiration.

My daughters had been my motivation.

But it was *me* who had done the brave work of reconciliation.

Chapter 22

Alliance

If your car is making a noise and you don't get it checked out, you can cause major damage to the engine. If Aphrodite's body said it hurt and she ignored it, she would be willfully harming herself in the moment while risking worse damage later. For someone who saw their body as their most prized possession—more than any car—ignoring would have been an unthinkable reaction to pain or fatigue. She absolutely would have listened. And I think she would have tried to figure out what the source was and fix it if she could. So, I vowed to pay attention to signals that were originating from my physical body and respond appropriately.

Now, I just needed to increase my daily awareness.

To truly embody Aphrodite, I also needed to know what she was thinking and use those thoughts as well. *I love this body. I cherish this body. This is my body and I love it! It's my favorite. It's my most prized possession. I honor this body. It's beautiful. It's perfect just like it is. I want to take care of it. It's done so much for me and I'm so grateful. I want to keep it working well.*

I tried to carry that loving desire to care for my body into my day and paid close attention to any and all signals that were coming through. After only hours of practicing this extreme level of awareness I was in awe of all the little ways the body communicates: hunger, fullness, fatigue, aches, pains, the urge to pee, itchiness, numbness, weakness, temperature changes, throbs, tingles, etc. Each one was telling me something, some vital information about what my body needed. And I had been ignoring them for so long!

These signals were my map. They were showing me exactly *how* to care for myself. I had been working to believe that my body was on my side, and I did believe that. Now I needed to be on its side as well; rather, I needed to be on *my* side. I needed to care for it the way I would if I loved it and prized it above all else, the way Aphrodite would. I needed to be its champion, its advocate.

As I stood, making breakfast for my kids, I could feel a slightly uncomfortable sensation in my hip and realized I was standing cock-eyed, so I balanced out my weight to relieve it.

As I sat doing homeschool with my daughters, I realized I was slumped over and it was creating a pulling sensation in my lower back, so I sat up straight.

As I checked my phone messages, I felt a discomfort in my neck from slumping my shoulders over, so I lifted my chest and shoulders to a more comfortable position while I tapped away.

After sitting for a bit, I realized my pelvis was hurting and my rear end felt uncomfortable, so I stood up for a minute. I just moved in place a little to get blood flowing and release any tension.

I felt thirsty, so I went and got a glass of water.

My neck and shoulders felt tense, so I took a minute to roll them and loosen up a bit.

When I noticed I needed to pee, I went. I did not sit there and hold it until I was finished with what I was doing. (This one cracked me up. I had no idea how often I held it rather than just going!)

When I took a break from a project, I realized I had been a little tense and hadn't been breathing properly, so I took a few deep breaths.

When I realized my back hurt, I grabbed my foam roller and rolled it out for 30 seconds.

When I felt tired midday, I rested for 20 minutes before starting my next activity.

With the exception of my 20 minute rest, none of these things took much time. Many of them didn't require any extra time at all, yet they made an enormous difference.

By resting before I got to that overly tired stage instead of pushing through, I was more productive and didn't feel like a zombie in the evening. The small pains and minor discomfort had been growing over the course of the day into something truly painful. At the end of the first day, I felt so much better than days past.

My body had been trying to tell me what it needed, but I hadn't been listening. Now, I was listening.

By answering the signals right away, my pain wasn't exacerbated.

I was fascinated by the way this worked. I also felt a bit chagrined. You see, my husband was naturally good at responding to his body's signals, but I never saw that as a positive thing. I remember so many times in our marriage when he would announce, "I'm tired. I'm going to go take a nap." Whether I actually said anything out loud about that or not, I always judged him for it. I really thought resting in the middle of the day was indulgent and lazy. I would think things like, *Well, it must be nice. Too bad all of us can't go rest whenever we want. Some of us have responsibilities.* Turns out, he had it right all along.

Now, it makes perfect sense to me to rest when you are tired, but I had completely missed that for most of my life. He seemed to understand this intuitively. And you know what? He has always had a healthy body and a good relationship with it. I vowed to pay more attention to the little ways that he cared for himself and learn from him.

I could really see how much sense all of this made and flabbergasted that I had missed something so basic for so long. Even so, I didn't suddenly become perfect at paying attention to my body. Some days I got totally distracted and wasn't present at all, especially if I was busy or out of my normal routine. When I did eventually remember to check in with my body I found I was hurting, stiff, uncomfortable, and really tired but just hadn't noticed. When that happened, I would immediately take time for some TLC.

Sometimes, like when I was riding on a plane, I just *was* uncomfortable and couldn't do much about it. That was okay too. Mostly, I just made the shift to recognizing that the signals my body sent truly *mattered*. I honored the signals. I didn't get frustrated at my body for feeling what it did. I felt compassion for its discomfort. I did what I could in the moment and made a point to take care of it as soon as I could without being frantic.

In the past, there were so many times when I could have listened to my body's signals but didn't for some reason. Often, I hadn't wanted to be awkward or to draw attention to myself. I also judged my body's needs, believing they made me weak. And I had unrealistic expectations about what it should be able to do in various settings. When it didn't meet those expectations, I got angry. Now, I saw all those signals as important and actively looked for ways to respond to them.

I recently went to a conference that involved long hours of sitting in folding chairs. Historically, whenever I did this I ended up hurting for days afterward. This time, I chose to sit in the back in an aisle seat. When I needed to stand up, I did. When I wanted to sit, I did. When I wanted to stretch a little, I did. As I stood, I shifted my weight back and forth to stay loose. When I sat, I would take a minute to massage my lower legs a bit to keep blood flowing. I was still discreet and didn't actively try to draw attention to myself, but I valued my body enough to care for it, even if the occasional person noticed. At one point I sat near some empty seats and stretched my legs across the empty ones for a change in position. These were little things, but they were little things I had not done before and they made a difference in how I felt both physically and emotionally. I was acting like my body was important and valuable to me, because it was.

And, when I took care of my body, it worked better.

Lesson 10: Aphrodite responds to her body's signals.

Understanding how loving it was to respond to the signals of our bodies made me think of my daughters and added another motivational layer to this work. I did not want them to treat their bodies the way I had treated mine. When I thought about them, it was easy to believe they were deserving of love and care, bodies included. I wanted them to care for all the parts of themselves. I wanted them to rest when they were tired. I wanted them to be healthy and full of vitality. I didn't believe they needed to push through pain or fatigue. I didn't think it was wise for them to ignore their bodies' signals. I wanted them to truly love their bodies and take care of them.

The only way they were going to learn how to actually do those things was if I modeled it for them. I could not push through fatigue all the time and then expect my kids to be good at resting when tired.

So, not only did I begin doing this work for me—training myself to respond lovingly to all my body's signals—I also began talking about it out loud so my kids could understand the reasons behind the actions.

I declared, "I'm feeling tired. I'm going to take care of myself by resting for a bit," in the presence of my daughters so they could see that was how it worked.

I would say, "I'm feeling hungry. I think I need some food. I'm going to take a break to get something before I get *too* hungry."

Or "I'm hurting, so I'm going to take care of myself by laying down for a bit."

And, a great one for any mama of young kids, "I need to pee, I'm going to go now and not hold it!"

Chapter 23

Holding the Line

I was doing *so* well with listening to my body's signals and responding throughout the day. I was becoming more aware of hunger and pain signals. I was getting more in touch with energy usage and generally feeling more connected to my body as a whole.

I had heard people speak of feeling "grounded" and never really knew what they meant. I realized *this* is what they meant. Being aware of what was happening in my body *right now* took my work of being present to a whole new level. Being aware of signals in the moment was helping me *be* in the moment. I felt connected to a particular place in time rather than being off somewhere in my head.

Perhaps best of all, we were operating as a team and I was beginning to be able to think, *"My body and I are one,"* and actually believe it.

Then, I hit a snag. We traveled up to San Francisco and connected with some family there for a couple of days. We had one day to explore the city on foot and I was determined to make the most of it. We walked and walked and *walked*. Up and down hills and all around the city. After a couple of miles, I dislocated a bone in my right foot (something that happens when my muscles fatigue and can't compensate for my connective tissue). I didn't want to head back yet so I just tied my shoe tighter and kept going. Then a bone slipped out in my left foot, so I tied that shoe tighter as well. As I kept going, more slipped out. When we finally got back to our hotel room, I sat on the bed and carefully removed my shoes. I had 5 bones out of place and both feet were swelling. It was painful, but I told myself it was *totally* worth it.

I changed my tune about that pretty fast. The bones did *not* want to go back in place or stay put. I tried and tried, but just couldn't get them to stay. I ended up needing to stay off my feet for 2 weeks. For the next several months I couldn't walk around at all unless the loosened joints were sturdily taped in place to stabilize them. I found I could no longer wear normal shoes without the bones slipping out and had to order special barefoot style ones. As of the time of writing this book, that is still my only footwear option.

During those weeks of recuperation, everything I had learned about responding to my body's signals was threatened. I *really* wanted to be able to be at peace with my body. I wanted to act and think the way Aphrodite did, the way a woman who loved herself would, but my disability was threatening this fledgling alliance.

Lying on my couch, unable to get up except for necessities, I thought about the work I had been doing with Aphrodite on body awareness. As I thought over the times it went well and the times it didn't, I could see a clear pattern. When I was "normal" tired, I was able to listen to my body's signals with a good attitude and I could see how that was the loving and wise thing to do. When it was more than that, when I came up against my lack of stamina that was a part of my disability, I got frustrated. I felt like I *should* be able to do more and that it wasn't fair. During those times, I found myself slipping back into the belief that my body was broken and that it was failing me. I would get really angry with my body during those times.

When I dislocated a joint and not only experienced high levels of pain but also couldn't do basic activities like typing, walking, or dishes, it was even worse.

I reasoned that Aphrodite didn't have to deal with *that*. *Her* body was perfect. *I* was different. It was harder for me to love this body than it would have been for her to love her body. I just couldn't quite wrap my mind around my Aphrodite having a less than perfectly functioning body.

As I thought about it more though, I realized, technically, she could have. Having the most beautiful body in the world didn't mean that it was the best functioning one. Beauty didn't necessitate perfect health. Maybe she *did* need more rest than the average woman, even if her reasons were different than mine.

I thought about all the women I knew. There were a few who had what might be considered perfect health, but most people I knew had *something* going on in their physical body—they had issues with their hormones, thyroid, or adrenals; they dealt with depression or anxiety; they had pain conditions or old injuries that flared up and caused pain.

I realized that while my condition was, perhaps, more extreme than most, I wasn't all that unique. And maybe, just maybe, Aphrodite could have been counted among the millions of women who had bodies that were less than 100% healthy. *What Would Aphrodite Do if she had some sort of limitation or physical symptoms outside of the normal function of a healthy body?* Specifically, I wanted to know what Aphrodite would do if she were in my place. What would she do if she had a disability that meant she got overly tired, experienced chronic pain, and sometimes ended up in bed with joints that wouldn't stay in place?

When I thought of it from the lens of her love, I could see the answer was the same. She would respond to her body's needs. *Technically*, I was doing that already. I rested when I had to and I stayed in bed when my pain was high.

But.

It wasn't just about what she would *do*.

It was about *how* and *why* she did those things.

I rested, but I didn't like it. I felt incredibly frustrated by it. It also often led me to think unkindly about my body.

Her?

Per usual, she felt love.

The *way* she responded was the key.

I could see it, but I was still confused by the *how*. *Tell me Aphrodite! How could you feel pain and still love your body? How could you be limited in your energy and still feel love? How could you love a body that was disabled and broken like mine?*

In my mind, my health issues were a clear, obvious *problem*, a barrier to really loving myself. Would Aphrodite have viewed a health issue as a problem? Would she have been angry at her body for it? Would she have been frustrated at her body for it? Would it have affected the love she felt?

No way. Not her.

It would be a logical impossibility. If it needs to be a certain way (like having abundant energy or not having a disability) in order to love it, then it wouldn't be genuine, unconditional love. As I sat there, I became convinced Aphrodite's love for herself was unconditional. It was something she felt all of the time. No matter what. Unconditional love was part of the essential makeup of the Aphrodite I had been imitating, though I hadn't realized it until now.

158

If I was going to go all the way with this; if I was going to think, feel, and act like Aphrodite; I would need to love my body *all the time* too.

Even when I was in pain.

Even when I was *still* resting beyond what I deemed appropriate or normal.

Even when I couldn't go do activities with my family because I needed to stay home and rest.

I would need to love my body even though it was disabled. I would need to care for it from a place of love, regardless of the reasons it needed care.

Lesson 10 (expanded): Aphrodite responds to all of her body's signals from a place of unconditional love, regardless of the origin of those signals.

My decision to respond to all of my body's signals, regardless of origin helped a ton. I realized I could still feel love, no matter what. I could choose to respond lovingly, regardless of what the origin of the signal was. Lying on my couch, I chose to think the same loving, caring thoughts about my body as I did the rest of the time. It was an exercise in awareness, self-control, and patience, but I found I could absolutely do this.

My body is on my side. It doesn't want to be in pain or disabled. I love this body no matter what. I want to care for this body. My body is my most prized possession. It is the only one I have.

This new resolve to love my body unconditionally was tested and tried in no time at all.

159

Chapter 24

A New Threat

As I journeyed with Aphrodite, I was also continuing to learn how to manage my health condition. I was constantly learning new things and trying new things. I found myself getting incrementally better month by month, though the progress was slow.

When my health had been at its worst, I was on a ton of medications, taking pills 10 times a day with several of those being heavy-duty prescriptions. I had been slowly working my way off them over the last couple of years, one at a time. I was now down to just one—a natural thyroid medication to manage my hypothyroidism.

I was so ready to be done with medication, trips to the pharmacy, and stupid phone calls back and forth between my doctor and pharmacy because both thought the other one was the reason my prescription wasn't ready. I was over it. I made a decision to go off that prescription, my very last one. I was *so* excited. I was also in a major hurry to shut that door and move on. So, I didn't consult with my doctor. I didn't properly wean myself, reasoning that would have taken *way* too long. I didn't get blood work done. I just stopped taking it.

Turns out, that was not a great idea.

A few days after I stopped taking the medication, I found I was exhausted. I was craving sweets. I felt moody. Yet, I just kept plugging away. I told myself, *My body is so much healthier! It's doing so much better. It just needs some time. It is going to figure this out and start producing enough of these hormones on its own any day now. We just need to wait it out.*

After a week, I stepped on the scale and saw I had gained 5 pounds.

Then 10.

Then 15.

Then 20.

At 25, I decided to go back on the medicine. Apparently my body was *not* going to figure it out and suddenly stop needing the assistance of the medication. Turns out, based on the research I did after the fact, that isn't typically how it works.

Months later, once I sorted out my dosage, 5 of those pounds dropped on their own. The other 20 decided to stay put.

When I began this work, I was in a healthy weight range. My only real barrier to loving my body was my own disordered thinking. Now? Now I was verifiably overweight by most charts.

This could be a problem.

My brain was starting to argue with all my loving thoughts. It was starting to use logic against me. *We really* are *fat now. This isn't in our head anymore. Those rolls are genuinely disgusting. You're clinically overweight. Fat is ugly.*

That seemed decidedly true, but did that *also* mean we couldn't love our body anymore? I had always thought so.

What Would Aphrodite Do? What would she do if she gained weight (for whatever the reason)?

I checked in with her.

161

The answer: Exactly the same thing that she was doing before.

The Aphrodite of my visions loved her body exactly the way it was. I couldn't see it changing just because the weight went up a bit. Unconditional love meant no matter what. It meant no conditions.

Lesson 11: Aphrodite loves her body unconditionally.

I thought about all the women in my life. I loved them dearly and saw beauty in each one, and not all were thin. I knew many who were curvy and voluptuous and absolutely stunning while others were thin and lean. Some were muscular and defined and some were "soft." I had friends who were underweight, some who were in a healthy weight range, and some who technically qualified as overweight. Even so, I never factored in their BMI when I thought of why I loved them. I did not love those with a lower weight more. I loved these women unconditionally because of who they were. They came in all shapes and sizes and it had never mattered one bit to me or to our friendship. So why should it matter in my relationship with myself?

I was beginning to see a pattern here. Whenever I checked in with Aphrodite to see what love would look like in the various situations I found myself, the answers were pretty much the same: Think loving thoughts and act in loving ways. There had yet to be a single external situation that changed that. Not my disability. Not my weight. I kept looking to find a legitimate reason to justify my hate, but kept coming up short. Unconditional love means *no matter what*. It means all the time.

So, I did the same things I had been doing at my lower weight: I spoke kindly to myself in my own mind. I acted from love. I cared for my body like it was my most prized possession. I avoided things that were harmful.

I was *strongly* tempted to go back to high intensity, calorie burning exercise. I reasoned I *needed* to do that to lose the weight. Yet, when I looked at how I felt without that (compared to how I had felt with it) I concluded it still wasn't loving. My body was already going through a lot trying to get back on track after the medication switch up. Not to mention all the daily stress of living with my condition. It didn't need the added stress of that kind of exercise. I continued to listen to my body and move it in ways that were loving. Sometimes I would catch myself trying to go a little longer with the mindset of calorie burning, but I just kept bringing my focus back to love.

At one point, I also found myself reconsidering my food choices from a diet mentality. *I mean, what does it matter? We're going to be fat no matter what we eat anyway. Might as well enjoy it.*

Well, hello red flags! Apparently there was still some part of my brain that connected "nourishing" eating with weight management. Since I had been eating nourishing foods and minimizing my emotional eating, I had easily been able to maintain my weight without feeling deprived. Now, when it seemed that it wasn't having any outward results, I wanted to throw in the towel and go back to eating junk!

More than ever before, I had to remind myself why I was eating the way I was. It wasn't about losing weight or maintaining weight. It was about loving this body, the only one I had to live in. It took more than a few reminders, including going back and remembering all the *other* reasons I didn't want to eat those things that didn't have to do with weight gain. I reminded myself about cancer, brain fog, hormonal balance, gut health, mental health, headaches, depression, anxiety, digestive discomfort, and everything else I could remember.

In the end, I decided it was *still* worth it to eat nourishing foods and avoid harmful ones. Even if I never lost a single pound, feeling good was worth it.

Choosing to continue to eat in loving, nourishing ways regardless of the number on the scale was one of the greatest acts of self-love I had ever performed. It was empowering and it helped me to really unlink healthful, nourishing foods from my weight in a way I hadn't before.

Honestly, gaining the weight was probably the best thing that could have happened to me, even though I didn't think so at the time. It forced me to do the next level of this work and learn to not only love my body at a healthy weight, but to *choose* to love it when it was overweight.

I learned that, ultimately, it is always a choice. There aren't some body sizes that are more lovable than others. There is just the choice to love the body I have or to not love it. My body was equally lovable at a small size as at a big size. It came down to what I would choose to do.

Now, I *really* knew that. Like, deep-down-in-my-bones knew that.

I could always choose love. No matter what.

I decided that day that I always *would* choose love. I would always choose to think and act in loving ways. That was the only way to truly imitate Aphrodite.

With that decision, not only was the war with my body thoroughly over, I knew it would stay that way. I had ushered in a lasting age of peace. Full armistice.

Chapter 25

Reclaiming the Land

The complete absence of fighting within myself was such a contrast to the life I had been living. Over the days and weeks after signing the peace treaty with my body, I found myself pondering war, peace, and fighting and what that had really produced. I came to a really profound and simple observation: True change never happens during war. The only thing war really brings is death and destruction. Growth, renaissance, and rebuilding always happen during times of peace. The war with my body had ended, and now I was ready for my renaissance.

As I looked over my life, there were so many areas that I had lost to the fighting, so many areas where the war with my body had spilled over and wreaked havoc. It was time to reclaim the land and take back what had been lost. It was time to rebuild the areas of my life that had been destroyed.

WWAD... in the bedroom?

I had been working to respond to my body's distress signals in order to remove pain...but what about pleasure? There was a whole other side to this conversation and I wondered if, perhaps, the best way to not feel *bad* in my body was to intentionally feel *good* in my body. I knew there were things that felt good to do—things like gentle movement, sitting in a hot tub, or getting a massage. These things were physically pleasurable, but I only did these things in response to pain and discomfort. I only got a massage to try to work painful knots out of my muscles, which was a medical necessity and far from pleasant in the moment. I stretched when I felt tight to relieve the pain. I sat in hot tubs or a hot bath to relieve soreness. I felt better afterwards, but they were always about bringing me back to neutral when I was in pain. I realized I could do things that felt good, even when I wasn't in pain, and those things could propel me to pleasure!

As I thought about Aphrodite loving her body, I really believed that she would engage in activities that felt good physically. She would show her body love by doing things that felt nice. I believed she would seek that out. Not just to relieve pain, but for the purpose of feeling physical pleasure.

I started practicing this in the areas I was comfortable with. I stretched before I ever got sore. I got massage therapy before I was majorly hurting. I even took time to massage my own calves and feet while watching TV just because it felt nice. I chose a comfortable seat when I could. I picked fabrics that felt good on my skin.

This was all really good progress and I kept looking for ways to up the pleasant sensations. But when I thought of "physical pleasure" it mostly made me think of sex.

I knew it was time to go there.

I have a body. That body is having sex.

This was true. It was also true that there wasn't much about my sex life that was goddess-like. Eating nourishing foods and physical pleasure, while both related to the physical body, existed on different planets as far as I was concerned.

I was *so* self-conscious of my body during sex. I would only have sex with the lights off to hide the cellulite, loose skin, and stretch marks. Touching my stomach or any other "squishy bit" was completely off limits and would pull me right out of the moment and into the familiar shame spiral. I was concerned about the wiggles and the jiggles and the bad angles. I made very little noise, feeling insecure about what it might sound like and not wanting to be "weird." In fact, I preferred as little touching of my body as mechanically possible. Every time my husband's hands touched my skin my brain was thinking about all the things I assumed he was thinking: that my body was gross and disgusting and fat. I truly thought that he was just suffering through my body looking and feeling like it did. I figured that having sex with me was likely better than having no sex at all and I reasoned he was simply smart enough to keep his mouth shut about something that might turn me off from intercourse entirely.

I know some women who do not enjoy sex. That wasn't true for me. I did enjoy sex with my husband and always had. However, when I really looked at it, I realized that I mostly loved the feeling of emotional connection, intimacy, and, if I'm honest, feeling like I did something nice for my husband. I did have physical sensations, and they were pleasant, but that had never been a primary motivation and that changed how I showed up in our sexual relationship. In truth, I had never even considered that physical pleasure could *be* a primary, or even a secondary, motivation for me to have sex. I had a belief that that was true for men, but not for women. However, I thought physical pleasure *would* have been a motivator for Aphrodite, or anyone who wanted their body to experience pleasant things.

Theoretically, that made sense, but I had a lot of resistance. I explored my current thinking regarding sex and what I found was...depressing. I was really repressed in this area and had some subconscious beliefs about it being bad to *really* enjoy sex. The general teaching I got about sex from growing up in the church was that it was "allowed" in marriage, but less holy than things like prayer. When I dug more deeply into this, I realized I thought of anything beyond what was necessary for emotional connection (which to me was kissing and missionary position sex) as impure.

Yet, I also knew God made my body. He put that bundle of nerves in that perfect spot that made sex enjoyable for me. On an intellectual level, I didn't believe it was bad to enjoy sex in my marriage, but there was a lot of hard-wiring there that kept getting in the way. Basically, I was in my head a lot during sex and mostly disengaged from the physicality of it. This wasn't surprising considering my past separation of mind and body.

What Would Aphrodite Do?

If she were like me, married and having sex with her husband, what would sex be like for her? What would she think when her husband touched her body? Lights on or off? What would intimacy be like for someone who loved and accepted their own body completely and didn't think it needed to change? What would sex be like for someone who had a specific goal of giving their body pleasure?

I did some visualization on what I imagined Aphrodite would be like in the bedroom. I imagined what sex would be like for a woman who loved her body completely and was not self conscious about any part of it. I visualized what sex would be like for a woman who wanted to feel pleasure in her body while having sex.

Then, I went and began to—slowly—put those visions into practice.

Let's just say...my husband noticed. He didn't know the reason for the change, but he saw the effects.

I started with simple things, like initiating sex rather than waiting for him to. Once, I "initiated" by getting naked and just laying on the bed to see what happened. (You can likely guess what happened.) The next time the lights were on when he initiated, I didn't insist on turning them off. I stopped blocking my husbands hands and, instead, leaned into his touch, choosing to believe he was touching me because he wanted to and that, if he didn't, he would stop.

It wasn't that I was suddenly doing all kinds of wild and crazy things with toys and swings and costumes, but I was engaging in my sexuality differently. I talked more openly, sharing things that felt good and things that didn't. I was less timid and more open to trying new things. I tuned into and focused on the pleasure I felt in my body.

These days, our sex life is a true source of pleasure for both of us.

I still believe sex is a source of emotional connection, however I've come to realize it also feels good in my body completely *apart* from any emotional connection. I know there are lots of strong opinions out there about sex inside a marriage and I don't want to even attempt to speak into any of that, let alone how this would apply outside of marriage. What I will say purely from personal experience is that lightening up has been nice. Within the context of my committed, monogamous marriage, sex can be about deep intimacy, but it can also just be about physical pleasure.

Sometimes, my husband and I have barely spoken, let alone had an emotional connection, for *days* due to busy schedules or travel, but we have a few minutes and have sex just because it's fun. I used to have a long list of how it was all "supposed to go," including all the deep, emotional connection that was supposed to come before. I believed I had to really feel "seen" to be sexual. Now, I just go with it. I let it be what it is. It has been really freeing to enjoy sex in all of its various expressions.

When I'm stressed out, in my head about work, or simply not feeling grounded in my body and really need to settle into the present moment, the things that work the best for me are mindfulness meditation, tai chi, or sex. During all of them, I become intimately aware of my physical body and the sensations happening there. All have amazing health benefits and are ways I can show love to my body. Overall, I just think sex is more fun, so I choose that option when I can.

Bedroom: reclaimed.

WWAD... in the bathroom?

One morning, I woke up, ready to start a day filled with learning to love myself. I set my feet on the floor and slowly shuffled to the bathroom, bleary eyed and only half awake. I used the bathroom, washed my hands, grabbed my toothbrush, and added some toothpaste. I shut the medicine cabinet and got my first look at myself. *Yikes.* My hair was crazy, my under eyes were puffy, and I generally looked pretty rough. After finishing with my teeth, I pulled out my brush thinking *I need to make myself semi-presentable so I don't terrify the family.* I laughed at myself, but I also started thinking about Aphrodite.

I tried to imagine what kinds of things Aphrodite would do in the bathroom. Would she have a beauty routine? I usually thought of my beauty routine as a "beautification" routine— something I did to make myself *more* beautiful. (Actually, before Aphrodite, I thought of it as what I did to make myself less ugly.) It was all about doing things to my appearance to improve it or cover up the parts I didn't like. I was only ever aiming for "presentable."

What sort of a beauty routine would the Goddess of Beauty have? She was already the standard of beauty, so no extra beautification necessary. Did that mean she did nothing? Well, no, I didn't think so. Her body was her most prized possession, so she would take care of it. When you use something, it gets dirty. If you care for it, you clean it. So, basic grooming would be a part of her routine for sure.

Beyond that, what does it look like to love and care for your face and body if you already think both are beautiful? The thing I thought of right away is that she would care for her skin. I imagined time spent cleansing, exfoliating, and nourishing with quality oils. Goddess of beauty or not, skin is fickle. If you don't take care of it, it shows. So, of course she would do that.

She would need to care for her hair as well. If she lived today, I imagined she would purchase quality hair products, without chemicals that would harm her body, but beyond that, washing hair is washing hair, right? Seems unremarkable as far as activities go.

Visualizing her washing her hair, I was drawn to her face; she was gently smiling. She seemed happy, which I thought was weird unless you're in a shampoo commercial. I never looked that happy while washing my hair. I realized that the physical actions might have been the same as what I was doing, but the thoughts and feelings would have been entirely different. Love would have transformed the experience entirely. I didn't necessarily have to do anything new or profoundly different in my beauty routine. Maybe I just needed to add a dash of love.

That evening, I scheduled some time to invest in my own beauty routine. I put myself in Aphrodite's headspace and practiced thinking of this as something I was doing for my body because I *already* loved it and thought it was beautiful and therefore wanted to care for it. I decided before I ever started that I would imitate Aphrodite and would not allow any negativity about my body to be in that bathroom with me. I would focus on caring for it. I decided to gently smile as I did each activity, think kind thoughts, and focus on feeling love.

I started by showering and washing my hair. Being positive here wasn't too hard. I have pretty great hair naturally, not too dry, not too oily, a good thickness. I just spent time appreciating it, which I had simply never thought to do before. My focus had always been on what was wrong with my appearance. Until that day, I had given very little thought to the things that were already great.

I shaved my legs and exfoliated my skin with a homemade sugar scrub. Then I toweled off and applied a homemade body butter on every area. I used this as a time to practice thinking kind thoughts about each and every part of my body. Some parts were easier than others.

I had some parts of me that I could appreciate for their physical appearance. Minus the years of atrophy from bed rest, I have naturally shapely, muscular legs. I've been told they are one of my best features. I wear a size 7 shoe, which makes shoe shopping easy as there are always lots of choices in that size. My shoulders and upper back have never been a source of loathing, they look pretty normal, so no complaints there.

For other parts, I couldn't quite say I liked what I saw, but I realized I could still engage in appreciation. I thought about all the things I could do with my hands—brush my daughters' hair, hold hands with my husband, drink a latte, make dinner for my family, even write a book—and felt gratitude for them. My arms were what I used to hug my daughters. My belly had carried two babies. My legs helped me walk, despite having less functionality than most people. That night, I just appreciated what I *did* have and what I *could* do. I knew that what I could do wasn't true for everyone. I decided to focus on the abundance of good rather than the things I lacked.

I spent some time on my nails. I have super strong nails that almost never break. I have nice, deep nail beds. I can grow my nails out, paint them, and they look like I have acrylics on. I don't always do that, but I took a minute to appreciate that I have the option.

I took time to do the things I knew to do in terms of facial cleansing, exfoliating, and clearing pores. As I looked at my skin, I took a moment to be grateful that I have never dealt with major acne. That was *such* a blessing in high school. My skin tone is pretty even, neither oily or dry. I've actually been told by many people that I have great skin, I just never took a minute to tell it *to myself*. That night, I did. I looked at my skin in the mirror and thought *I've got good skin*.

I looked at my features in the mirror and tried to see what I could appreciate there. My features are proportionate, delicate. My nose is the right size for my face. Not too big, not too small. When I really thought about it, I realized I kind of liked *liked* my nose. This "liking" felt weird, but was true. In fact, nothing about my appearance was that terrible. I wasn't going to stop traffic with my looks, but I looked all right. Cute even.

I think that picking apart my appearance and being negative about my looks had somehow seemed like the "right" thing to do. Everyone I knew picked apart their appearance, so I had too. Looking in the mirror and liking my appearance seemed completely self-absorbed. I equated complimenting my own appearance with vanity.

Was it vain to like my face?

Was it conceited to love what I saw in the mirror?

Was it self-absorbed to think that, perhaps, I was lovely?

173

I have talked to a lot of people about this concept and many think that, yes, it is vain, conceited, or self-absorbed. So they continue to hate their face.

All I can say is this: That night as I went over each body part and the roles they played in my life, it didn't feel vain.

It felt like peace.

It felt like kindness.

It felt like basic human decency to give my own appearance the same measure of love as I would the face of someone else I loved.

I love my daughters' faces. I love my husband's face. I love the faces of my family members. I love the faces of my friends. When I see those faces, I feel so much joy. I can genuinely look at their faces and say, *I love this face!* and totally mean it. Now, I *do* think that many of these faces are objectively lovely, but I don't love their faces for that reason. I love their faces because they are *their* faces. That is what my daughters, my husband, and my friends actually look like. I love *them*, so I love the faces they have.

I realized I could love my face simply because it was *my* face. If I loved me, and my face was part of me, the part that I showed to the world, then I would love it too. It was mind bending to realize that loving my face had very little to do with the face itself. It had nothing to do with wrinkles, dark circles, grey hair, age spots, eye color, or the shape or size of anything on my face. It had everything to do with my choice to love it for its own sake, the same way I would love the face of a loved one who was precious to me. Loving my own face meant deciding *I* would be precious to me as well.

174

My new thought when I looked at my face in the mirror was: *This is me. This is my face. I love me. I love this face. It is the only one I have and it is precious to me.*

This was *not* easy. My brain had a lot to say about all of this. I just kept saying these and similar things on purpose any time I looked in the mirror.

I'll admit, I did feel more beautiful after my time in the bathroom. I didn't do anything major and it didn't take too long, but I felt amazing afterwards. I was still me, but a well cared for version of me. My skin looked healthy and fresh.

All my negative thoughts about my face weren't gone after one intentional session in the mirror, but I found that right away there were some legitimately grateful thoughts in the mix as well. There were lots of things that I did like about my body once I thought about it.

I decided that, from here on out, I *would* think about it. I would use my beauty routine as a time to appreciate, rather than criticize, the body that I had.

I still don't love wrinkles, but I also don't wish I had a different face. This one is mine and I have *decided* I like it. I'm not self absorbed. I don't sit around with thoughts that are completely consumed with my appearance. But, when I see my face in the mirror, I don't feel disgust anymore. I think, *This is my face. It's mine and I like it.* I don't ever call it an ugly face in my own mind. I see no benefit to hating it, so I don't.

This is not about comparison. This isn't me saying "me" more than "you." This is me being appreciative of the body I have, rather than criticizing it. This is me making a choice to look in the mirror and experience love rather than hate.

With the choice to leave hate in the hallway, the bathroom went from being a room that I wanted to avoid to one I actually enjoy being in. Time alone in the bathroom is sought-after and refreshing. Rather than equating the bathroom with criticism, I equate it with appreciation and with love.

Bathroom: reclaimed.

WWAD…at the closet?

Getting dressed in the morning was an activity that had become completely unenjoyable due to my negative thinking about my body. It was time to reclaim the square foot of space in front of my closet as well as shopping trips and wearing clothes in general.

Up until this point, when I visualized Aphrodite, I mostly imagined her wearing a toga. Even though she represented so much more for me than the mythical woman who started all of this, I still originally visualized her sporting a traditional Greek wardrobe. I'm no expert, but I didn't imagine there were a whole lot of options in terms of toga choices. I suppose there would have been various qualities of fabric, different colors, and adornments that could be added. I imagined she would have chosen quality, lovely items. I imagined she would have loved what she wore.

If I wore a toga, I would probably be thinking the same things I thought about everything else I wore: how fat it made me look. The biggest factor for whether or not I would buy an item of clothing was not whether I loved it, but about whether it made my figure look slimmer or heavier. There are several dress styles that I actually like a lot, but I never wear because they accentuate the wrong parts of my figure and make me look heavier than I actually am, which in my book is to be avoided at all costs.

When I thought about it, I determined togas *are* kind of frumpy. Yet, if you knew your body was beautiful, would that matter? A lovely body is a lovely body no matter what adorns it. Aphrodite would have rocked it anyway. If she was 100% unshakably convinced of her beauty, and loved her body no matter what, she could have worn a burlap sack around and not felt bad about how it affected her shape. If Aphrodite looked a little frumpy in her toga, it would have been the toga's fault, not the fault of her body.

You know, not that long ago, it was normal for people to have the majority of their clothing made to their specifications. Or to have items tailored to fit. Can you imagine how different that would be? Up until this point, if I tried on something and it didn't fit right, I blamed my body. I often told people that my body was oddly sized and that made it hard to buy clothes that fit—just one more evidence of my body failing me. I had a wide waist and narrow hips, which made women's pants either too tight in the waist or too loose through the hips. Carrying weight in my stomach meant a lot of dresses and shirts were a big nope. Yet, here is what I deduced: If Aphrodite tried on something that didn't fit, the only thing that would mean is *it didn't fit*. Neutral. Nothing to do with her. No negative thoughts about her body. Everything to do with the garment itself.

I took this experiment a little further and tried to imagine that Aphrodite was alive today and wearing clothing typical to this era. My mind didn't produce any specific style, but it did vividly imagine her thoughts and emotions. I think she would have *enjoyed* getting dressed. It would have been fun picking out items to adorn her body. I don't think, "Does this make me look fat?" would ever have crossed her mind. I think the singular question would have been, "Do I love this?" That may have included how it looked *on* her body, sure, but the answer would have been separate and completely unlinked from her love *for* her body.

There would have been no need to hide her body. No need to try to downplay anything, but also no need to try to show anything off either. I was flooded with the imagined feelings of confidence she would have felt when standing in front of the mirror, looking at a body she loved and prized just as it was.

With my recent weight gain, I had started buying clothes that were oversized and unshapely, the sole purpose being to hide the additional fat on my body. I had basically decided that I was only allowed to wear loose clothing because I was too fat for anything else. I knew on some level that this wasn't true, because I saw women of every size wearing clothes that played to their strengths, looked awesome on them, and obviously made them feel great. I remember marveling at women who were clearly overweight and also loving their style and wearing flattering clothes they loved.

I was allowed to do this too.

I started by going through my closet and getting rid of the items that made me feel rotten about my appearance, either because they did not work well with my current body shape or because they were too small. I didn't have the budget to do a complete overhaul all at once, but I started making changes where I could. I got rid of the pieces that were truly awful even if it left fewer options, realizing I would rather wear a few well fitting things that I loved than have a ton of variety. I slowly started buying pieces I loved that showed off my body a little more. I made it a point to only buy and wear things I loved.

Again, like so many things before, a lot of the transformation happened in my mind. Some of it was simply changing what I thought of when I got dressed. Instead of asking, "What would hide my stomach fat?" I tried to think as if my body was perfect and didn't need to be hidden, even if I was wearing the same things I had before. I tried to think like Aphrodite when I looked in the mirror, which would *not* have centered on an inventory of flaws. While I dressed, I thought of my day and the things I would do wearing the clothes. I was grateful I had clothes at all.

Then, I worked to make my confidence match the love by acting like Aphrodite *in* my clothes. I stood up straighter. I stopped crossing my arms over my stomach to hide it. When I sat on the couch, I resisted the urge to put a pillow on my lap to hide my body. I stopped insisting on being at the back in photos. I stopped commenting on how my body looked to my friends.

I tried to think like Aphrodite when I shopped for clothing too. If it didn't fit or didn't look nice, I told myself there was nothing wrong with my body, there was something wrong with the item. Bodies are not designed for clothes; clothes are designed for bodies. And just because I tried something on from a rack (that was designed for no body in particular) and it didn't fit well, didn't mean there was anything wrong with my body. Eventually, I didn't feel the need to blame anyone or anything. If it didn't fit, it simply didn't fit.

I made a mental decision that sizes no longer mattered. So much of my self worth hung on the number printed on the tags inside my clothes. Tags that no one would see but me. Tags that, as I shopped around more, proved to be arbitrary. A size 8 in one brand is a size 6 in another, and often a size 10 in another! Yet, for all my life, I felt bad about myself for buying the 10 and great about myself for buying the 6, even if I was an 8 in 95% of clothes. A number as meaningless as that shouldn't get such a huge say in how I felt about myself. It didn't matter what the number was unless I decided it mattered. I decided it didn't! It only mattered if I loved it. Regardless of my ability to

179

find clothing that fit just right, I committed to loving the body I had, no matter what. (BTW, when you get clothes designed specially for your body, there aren't any numbers.)

I still don't shop for clothing as a form of entertainment. I am still not overly concerned about fashion. The biggest change is that I don't use clothing against myself anymore. If I am going to shop, I go with the expectation that I'll find pieces that I love that look great on my body. I can genuinely say that I *enjoy* clothes shopping when I go. I like getting dressed. I like the things in my closet.

Closet: reclaimed.

WWAD…at the beach?

The summer before I "met" Aphrodite, my family and I took a trip to the beach. (This was right after I began eating solid food again after my stomach paralysis issue and I was beginning to gain back some weight.) It was one of our first beach days after moving to Southern California and I hadn't been in a swimsuit for a while. I inventoried the options in my closet and tried on a bikini I had owned for a couple of years. I was considering wearing it because I was pasty white and could use some sun. But, I had bought it when I was at my lowest weight and it was fitting a little differently now. I asked my husband if he thought I could still pull off a bikini with my current level of stomach fat.

He's an honest guy, so he told me the truth, "It's borderline."

I thought so too, which is why I had asked his opinion in the first place. I was right on the border between the bikini looking good and it just making me look overweight. I opted for my one-piece, which would hide the stomach fat well and be slimming. I shoved the two-piece back in my closet for a possible future when I could wear it again. I wasn't self-conscious in my one-piece, but it wasn't really what I wanted to be wearing. I was bummed to not be able to get the sun I wanted. I spent a lot of the day sad that I no longer had a two-piece swimsuit kind of body, lamenting my growing waistline.

Now, in the present, I was getting ready for another day at the beach. I looked at my one-piece and I looked at my two-piece. I wasn't sure what to do. Once again I wanted to wear a two-piece because I wanted to get some sun, but if I was borderline too heavy for a two-piece before, I most definitely didn't have the body for it now. I was still carrying around 20 extra pounds and a lot was in my mid-section.

American culture has a pretty clear cut definition of what a proper beach body is, and it wasn't mine. There were certain bodies that could wear bikinis and certain ones that couldn't. There were certain bodies that also needed shorts or a cover up over their one piece swimsuit. I put myself in the latter category.

What Would Aphrodite Do?

Well, I assumed she would do whatever she wanted. Her body was the epitome of beauty, so she had nothing to prove and nothing to hide. She could show stomach or not. She had done so for the statue, so the beach wouldn't be much different. Either one would have been fine *for her*. I knew I was meant to be imitating her, but we weren't *actually* the same size or in the same body, so I had to really weigh the cultural expectations and my actual body against the concepts and principles of self love.

In the end, I decided to just do what I had been doing and pretend like I actually was Aphrodite, regardless of all the other noise between my ears. We lived in Southern California and went to the beach a few times a month in the summer. I was ready to reclaim this part of my life for love and stop feeling ashamed of my body every time I went to the beach. And, I wanted some sun on my belly!

Bikini it is.

Enter the most abject terror I felt on this journey to date. Eek! I made a decision to do it anyway. I was so tired of being concerned about these sorts of things and I was committed to my WWAD method wholeheartedly. I would imitate Aphrodite if it killed me, and for the first time I felt like I was at genuine risk of that. My heart was beating out of my chest and I felt like I was on the verge of a panic attack at the prospect of waltzing around in a bikini in front of people, even if they were all strangers. I wasn't even brave enough to tell my husband about my plan—not that Aphrodite would announce to the world that she was wearing a two piece anyway—so I hurried to put the suit on and my clothes over it before I could change my mind. I took a deep breath, opened the bedroom door, and strode out of the room like Aphrodite, just going about her business as usual, even though I was anything but.

Standing in the warm sand at Venice Beach, I definitely delayed the reveal a bit. I left my clothes on while I got everything all perfectly situated for our claimed area of sand even though everyone else had already stripped down. I took some extra time to get everything *just right*, and to make just *one more* check of my phone for messages before stowing it. Enough. Grabbing the fabric of my tank top, I pulled it over my head while everything in me screamed *Don't do it! Danger! Danger!* But I did it. My husband looked a little surprised, but thankfully, didn't comment.

I had to work *soooooo* hard to be loving in my mind, walking around the beach in my two-piece. My kids' very honest remarks and observations about how I typically didn't wear a two-piece and how very white my stomach was didn't help.

I asked, *What Would Aphrodite Do?* And tried to answer them the way I imagined she would, "You're right. It *is* really white, that is why I wanted to wear this suit today. I'm going to let it get a little sun."

As I lay in the warm sun, soaking up the rays on my stomach, I checked in with Aphrodite. *What Would Aphrodite Do? What would she think about while lying on the beach?*

Despite being the Goddess of Beauty, the Aphrodite of my mind was not self-absorbed. So, I didn't think she would sit around thinking about her body the whole time, no matter how beautiful it was. I realized that sort of fixation and obsession would be similar to the disordered Thoughts I had, albeit from a different angle. I thought about my body so much because I was insecure. Aphrodite was completely secure in her beauty, so I didn't believe she would have been thinking about it every second of the day.

I reasoned that a woman who loved and accepted her body, but wasn't obsessing or comparing, would think about *the beach,* which is what the day was really about. So, that is what I did. I thought about the beach. I enjoyed my time. I stayed present in the moment. I read a book. I watched my kids playing in the sand. I oohed and aahed over their sand creations and the creatures they found. I talked to my husband. I just focused on everything else and did my best to not think at all about my swimsuit, how many pieces it was, or how I looked in it.

I did find myself occasionally observing the other beach goers, their bodies and their swimsuit choices. I would love to say that was purely out of curiosity, and that was part of it, but it was also a little bit of comparison for the sake of validation (I can admit that). Looking back, choosing the two-piece that day actually ended up being a good thing. I saw that there were lots of women of all ages who were heavier than me and sporting two-piece suits as well. And they didn't seem bothered.

In college, I took a trip to Romania to do humanitarian work. On a day off, some friends and I visited a natural hot spring. Settling into the hot spring in our super conservative suits, observing everyone nearby, I wondered if they even sold one piece suits in Romania!

From what I saw, every body was a beach body there—old bodies, young bodies, saggy bodies, firm bodies, thin bodies, fat bodies. Apparently, they were all two-piece worthy, because they were all wearing: *two-pieces*! Even the male bodies, regardless of shape or size, were unapologetically Speedo bodies.

Turns out, they were all just *human* bodies.

And, evidently, you can put whatever swimsuit you want on a human body.

Fascinating.

These days I wear what I want, but it is still a fully conscious choice to think loving thoughts about my body when I wear a two-piece. These thoughts aren't automatic yet, but I hope they will be someday. I do find it is getting easier with repetition.

Beaches and swimsuits are being reclaimed for love. And I'm okay that it is still a process. No one said the reclaiming of all these things had to happen quickly.

Beach: reclaimed.

Chapter 26

Cooperation

It was so empowering to know that I could choose to love my body at any weight. To really, *really* know that it had never been about weight. That was especially great because my body did not seem inclined to let go of the extra 20 pounds I was carrying, so Aphrodite and I just kept on truckin'. I kept doing what I was doing while my thyroid regulated and my body recovered from the shock of going off, then on, the medicine so suddenly. After a few months, when everything seemed regulated and back to normal, I faced a new question.

Just because I *could* love my body at any weight, did that mean I had to keep the extra 20 pounds? I had wanted peace with my body more than a thin body, and I now had that peace. I felt the love I had always wanted to feel, but did that mean I *shouldn't* lose the weight? Or *could* I lose it now? I wasn't sure.

I was firmly committed to loving *me* no matter what weight I was at, but I didn't like carrying around the extra weight. I was uncomfortable in my body in a way that didn't have to do with body image. It was harder to move. It was more difficult to find clothing that was comfortable because a lot of the weight was in my stomach. When I did pilates, the stomach rolls restricted movement. When I exercised, there was a lot of moving and shaking and my inner thighs chafed. I also knew that carrying around any extra weight made things harder on my joints. Not to mention the studies linking extra fat, especially stomach fat, with numerous health issues.

It honestly didn't seem healthy or loving to keep the extra weight, but I wasn't sure how to lose weight in a healthy way. After all the changes I had made in the name of love, I hoped the weight would come off naturally.

It didn't.

I was so incredibly afraid to mess up this good thing that I had going. I didn't want to be 20 pounds overweight, but I also didn't want to fall back into disordered eating again. It wasn't worth that. I did not want to trigger all the obsessive thoughts.

It felt like I had to choose to be overweight and at peace with my body, or to diet and fall into disordered eating. I was taught that if you restrict food, if you diet, if you weigh yourself too much, or try to lose weight, it will lead to an unhealthy relationship with food.

That was definitely true *in my past*. My attempts to lose weight were always decidedly unloving. I was often eating such low nutrient foods that my body didn't have what it needed to function. I associated weight loss with fatigue, brain fog, and generally feeling terrible. I remember in college I was so desperate that I even bought diet pills despite knowing they were harmful. I would be excited over things like the stomach flu because it would lead to weight loss—both from getting all the recently eaten food out of my stomach before it could turn into fat and because I wouldn't want to eat for several days after. I had not cared for the body I was in. I just wanted it to be thin regardless of the damage done or what it cost in terms of health and wellbeing.

For a while, I decided it was better to keep the 20 pounds. I avoided doing anything even remotely associated with weight loss out of fear that I would end up back there again. I didn't weigh myself. I didn't think about calories. None of it. I still focused on nourishing foods and didn't overeat to the point of discomfort, but that was about it.

Yet, as I continued to have great success with my WWAD method, I wondered if it might be different now. I was already "restricting" my food in many ways, like my choice to not eat sugar because I didn't feel like it was loving. That was technically a food restriction, but it came from love so I didn't *feel* restricted. I simply felt love. That closely resembled diet related activity, but it hadn't triggered anything negative or the return of the Thoughts. In fact, it had led to a more positive way of thinking because I was doing it from love. Every time I avoided a food I was thinking, "I love myself too much to eat that," and reinforcing patterns of love.

I had grown so much during this time with Aphrodite. Things really were different now. *I* was different now. I wasn't at war with my body anymore. I was listening to it and responding to its needs with love. I could think about it without feeling self-loathing. With the help of Aphrodite, I no longer felt a desire to harm myself in any way.

Perhaps my future didn't have to be a repeat of my past.

I spent some time researching the updated science of weight loss to make sure I wasn't going to unintentionally hurt my body in any way. Then, I gave it a go.

I made changes to my diet: what I was eating and when I was eating it. I was still eating foods that were nourishing and I wasn't restricting calories, but from my list of nourishing foods, I focused on the ones that would encourage my body to tap into its own fat stores. I never told myself I couldn't eat other foods and I didn't label them as bad, wrong, or off-limits. I just thought about how loving it would be to let my body get back to where it was comfortable. It felt loving to pass on those foods for the sake of my greater overall wellbeing.

I adjusted the timing of meals—and the timing of when I ate certain nourishing foods based on their makeup—to help my body become more insulin sensitive and more able to access fat stores for energy. This was so different from when I used to skip meals or go without food as a punishment. This felt more like a puzzle. I was simply adjusting pieces and seeing if it "clicked" for my body. It was all totally fine.

My first real obstacle was the scale. I used to dread stepping on the scale. It felt like Russian Roulette. I was waiting to see the number to determine what would come next. Would the number go up and produce an onslaught of shame and loathing? Or would it go down and let me feel good about myself for the day? It was always a gamble. I have heard you shouldn't weigh yourself everyday because it will lead to disordered thinking about your body.

What Would Aphrodite Do? Would she weigh herself?

This was a fascinating thought for me. I had always weighed myself because I was so focused on monitoring if I was losing weight, which was always of paramount importance. Weight was the central point that my life revolved around. Aphrodite loved herself just like she was, so would she weigh herself?

I concluded she wouldn't have any reason to *avoid* weighing herself. Regardless of what number she saw, she would love herself. If love was always the emotional response, regardless of the number, then the number would just be…a number. It would just be information—data. In that context, I could see how weighing herself, or myself, regularly would be a phenomenal tool for self-love. It would give me feedback on how my body was doing. Regularly tracking weight could show me things like how my thyroid was functioning, if I was retaining water, or if something was causing my body to start storing fat unnecessarily, or conversely, if my body was dropping weight when I wasn't trying to make that happen. It could be an early warning system and a way to keep an eye out for my body's wellbeing. While trying to release the extra weight, it would give me feedback on how the choices I was making were affecting my fat stores.

For the sake of love, I started weighing myself most days. I chose to think of the number as data with a commitment to love myself no matter what number popped up. I observed trends and saw how my weight slowly went up a few pounds each month with my hormonal cycle, then would drop them all at once when my hormones shifted. I saw little fluctuations that had nothing to do with fat stores and everything to do with hydration and how recently I had used the bathroom.

I observed with utter fascination how my kids use our scale. They get so much joy from it and I tried to tap into their childlike wonder. They sometimes go weeks or months without even remembering it is there, but sometimes they get on these kicks where they weigh themselves repeatedly throughout the course of a single day. They weigh when they get up, then they go drink a bunch of water and weigh again. Then they eat breakfast and see how much their food weighed. They weigh after they use the bathroom to see what came out. They weigh at the very end of the day to see how much all their food and water weighed for the day. And you know what? It doesn't lead to disordered thoughts or disordered eating. They just think it is *fun* and *interesting*. They find the scale entertaining. I was amazed to find that I could use it the same way. The number on the scale could just be...*interesting*.

I found this was true of so many things related to weight loss. There were things I avoided because I had associated them with shame and self-loathing, but in this season of loving weight loss, I redeemed each one of them for love.

I found I could track food if I wanted, and found that *was* loving in seasons where I was trying to see how various foods felt in my body. I didn't track calories, but rather I looked at what I was eating and when I was eating it to see what I could observe and learn. I found that some foods made me feel tired and sluggish, while others gave me energy. Some affected my digestion negatively and some sat really well. Writing it down helped me observe trends over time and figure out which things worked best in my particular body.

I found I could make a plan in advance for what I was going to eat without associating it with a diet plan. I was collecting data to see how various foods and eating times affected my body's function, and this allowed me to collect more accurate data. That made the process quicker and easier because I just followed the plans and observed the results. For a mama with a lot going on, that sometimes felt more loving than having to choose in the moment.

I could even weigh food if I wanted. The weight and volume of food consumed would just be data and information. I didn't often do that, but I realized I *could* and it wouldn't be disordered if I was doing it for the sake of data collection. My kids could weigh and measure their food for a week just out of curiosity to see how many pounds of food they ate and would probably find that fascinating.

All of the things I used to negatively associate with dieting, when separated from the negative thoughts I would be thinking about them, were really just ways of tracking information and being intentional. They used to feel awful to me because I had used them as ways to punish and deprive myself of good things. I used them from a place of self-hatred with the primary motivation being to change myself into something I found acceptable. Now, I was committed to loving myself no matter what, so they went back to being what they had always been: tools. Like all tools, they were optional. I could use them if there was benefit and leave them if not.

With Aphrodite's love guiding all my choices, I found that the process of weight loss wasn't exciting or dramatic in any way. Honestly, it wasn't even that hard. Before Aphrodite, the most difficult part had been dealing with the mental and emotional beat downs I gave myself when my body didn't do exactly what I wanted it to do precisely when I wanted it to do it. Now, if it wasn't releasing weight, I simply got curious. I asked, *Why?* I approached my body with compassion and worked *with* it.

I listened. I paid attention.

I stopped anything that felt like it wasn't working. I made small adjustments.

I wasn't in a hurry.

With this method, I lost the weight I set out to lose and then some. I actually missed several days of weighing because I was traveling and got a couple of pounds below my goal weight without realizing it. I could have easily kept going, nourishing and loving my way to greater fat loss, but my facial wrinkles were starting to look a little more prominent, so I stopped because I actually *wanted* to stop losing weight, not because I couldn't keep doing what I was doing. I could have kept going, but I chose to gain back a couple of the pounds I had dropped, feeling like I genuinely looked better at a slightly higher weight and carrying a percentage or two more of body fat. That realization almost knocked me over. Weight gain had always been what happened when I gave up and threw away restrictions. Going up two pounds didn't really change much about what I was eating. I didn't suddenly indulge in everything in sight. It was just a slight tweak. And then, when I got where I wanted, another slight tweak to maintain rather than gain or lose.

Since then, I have easily maintained my ideal weight. I actually think of it more as a weight range of about five pounds. I typically have a three pound fluctuation that happens naturally over the course of the month that is related solely to hormones. I weigh myself most days and attach no self-worth to the number that pops up. I use stepping on the scale as a time to practice loving myself unconditionally. I observe what is going on and make slight changes to my diet if I start moving too far out of that range in one direction or the other.

Just like with eating a salad, *why* we do things matters. The same principle applies to *all* things weight loss.

I get to decide what to eat, when to eat it, how much to have, whether or not to track my food, and if I step on the scale. They are all choices I make, and I also get to make choices about what I think when I do those things and that makes all the difference in the world. In the same way, I found I could simply choose if I wanted to be in a heavier body, or a lighter body.

In the past I wanted to lose weight because I hated myself. I thought that being at a lower weight would resolve the hatred. I was mean to myself through the whole process. This time, I loved myself through the whole process. I had proven to myself that I could and would love myself no matter what I weighed or what size clothes I wore. I chose to lose the weight simply because I *wanted* to. I chose to do it because it felt like the most loving choice. And that transformed everything about the experience.

I wasn't trying to impress anyone. I didn't need to add anything else to be happy with my life. I had great friends who loved me for me, my business was growing, my marriage was stronger and more fun than it had ever been, my daughters were growing into amazing people. I liked my life. I didn't *need* to lose weight to be happy or feel loved. I just wanted to. I felt better in a thinner body. Everything—walking, sitting, stretching, moving—was easier and more comfortable in a thinner body. Being in a thinner (lighter) body was easier on my joints and better for my condition. It was better for my overall health to lose the weight.

So, I did.

I loved myself right into my ideal weight.

This, more than anything else, was how I *knew* that I had accomplished what I set out to do—learning to act like a woman who loved her body. This was the final test. The last hurdle. If I could show love to my body through losing weight, I felt like I could love my body through anything.

It worked. My WWAD method actually worked. I had overcome the things I set out to overcome. I had figured out what I needed to figure out. I felt confident when I talked to my girls. I knew how to teach them to love their bodies.

Together, Aphrodite and I had done it.

Part 4: Loving My Whole Self

Note to Reader

While I have done my best to present these lessons from Aphrodite in a logical order, the actual process I went through was decidedly less linear. I was asking myself What Would Aphrodite Do? *all day long, in any and every situation. Sometimes I spent long chunks of time applying a single lesson before taking in more. Sometimes while working to apply a lesson in one area of my life, I was simultaneously learning another lesson in a different area.*

While the war with my body, mealtimes, and movement were my top priorities, I looked to Aphrodite for more than help with my body image and disordered eating patterns. Aphrodite loved every bit of herself. Part 4 is a compilation of additional lessons I learned from Aphrodite that have to do with loving my whole self.

All of these lessons happened after Chapter 19 (when I ended the war with my body). Most of them happened after Chapter 24 (when I gained the weight) and before Chapter 26 (when I lost the weight). You'll notice that I am clearly still in process here, not having found the confidence of Chapter 26 yet.

Chapter 27

Practice Love

Only a week before the trip to the museum where I met Aphrodite, I sat down to write out my New Year's resolutions. I came away with three pages of single-typed text detailing what I planned to do differently in the new year. If I succeeded at implementing all of them, I believed I would be able to feel genuinely good about myself. If I succeeded, I would also be an entirely different person, living an entirely different life. I would be without flaws in my own eyes and (I assumed) the eyes of the world, doing 48 hours of work in 24 hours of time and executing everything I set my hands to with superhuman perfection. In summary: I just needed to be perfect.

My thoughts about my body were much improved, but I still had other thoughts: *I'm so stupid. What's wrong with me? I'm a bad Mom. I should have this figured out by now. I'm not good enough. I'm a fraud. I'm awkward. I'll never succeed.* Those had nothing to do with my body and everything to do with *me*.

Myself.

Who I was.

My identity.

The negative thoughts about my body had been at the extreme forefront of my consciousness. With those diminishing, I could finally see clearly what was lurking behind. Not loving my body was simply one aspect of not loving myself, because my body is a part of *me*. I couldn't isolate love and care to one part of me, my body, while hating the rest.

Once I consciously identified my negative thoughts about myself, it was easy to see I had been fighting *this* war for a long time too. I tried to think about it the way I had with my body, but failed to pinpoint a specific time when this started for me. There wasn't a single moment when shame for who I was entered. Rather, it seems like it grew gradually over time.

It was hard for me to recall a time when I didn't feel like I needed to be better or different, even when I was very young. I couldn't remember a time when I felt perfect and whole. I am convinced that it was true at some point, because I cannot imagine a child born with self-hate. It had been a very long time though. I fundamentally believed I was not good enough.

I needed to be better.

I needed to be *different*.

In childhood, I remember genuinely believing I was somehow different from my family and that I didn't fit in with them. I reasoned that if I didn't fit in with my own family, then I didn't fit in anywhere.

I felt like a walking contradiction. I talked too much in some situations and too little in others. My family labeled me as bossy and argumentative, but I also hated conflict and seldom stood up for myself. I was Valedictorian of my high school class, but still thought of myself as dumb—I believed I had fooled everyone into thinking I was intelligent when I wasn't. I had successes and achievements I could list, but I never felt like they were good enough. I reasoned that, were I from a larger town or had I gone to a larger school, I wouldn't have even had those things. Still, I continued to try to *prove* that I was enough, that I was acceptable, that I was valuable.

The problem with not feeling good enough and attempting to earn worth is that it can masquerade as humility and hard work. Those are two characteristics that I had always thought of as positive. Throughout my life, I worked ridiculously hard to get good grades, please my coaches, be a model employee, and not get in trouble with my parents. That looks good from the outside, but no one asked me *why* I did it. No one noticed that I was trying to prove I was good enough. *I* didn't even recognize that was what was happening. I deflected compliments, downplayed my achievements, and would strive to improve on successes. I saw this as modesty rather than telling the truth about what it really was: an inability to believe I had done anything worth praising.

The bottom line? I did not like myself.

Thanks to my success with Aphrodite, I knew I could think and act differently in *any area* of my life. If I wanted to change this obsession with perfection and learn to think, feel, and act the way a woman does who loved her whole self as well as her body, I could. Aphrodite knew how and she could teach me.

In truth, if I saw a genuine chance of "winning" this war with myself, I might have kept going, because I really *did* think being different might be best. Yet, despite my best efforts, I wasn't gaining any ground in this war against me. It was time to end it. It was time to end the hate, lay down my weapons, and find a way to make peace with myself.

Before Aphrodite, I was hard on myself because I thought I *should* be hard on myself. I thought that was how you got better. When I was an athlete and I would make a mistake, the coach would yell at me. That was how I knew what I did wrong. That was how I knew I needed to work harder. Calling out wrongs felt like step-one to improving and becoming better.

This was why I was always fighting myself, always yelling at myself. I believed that the prerequisite to personal growth was taking inventory of my flaws, weaknesses, and shortcomings and that the avenue to change was paved with harsh words. I needed to "whip myself into shape." I needed to push myself. I needed to shame myself until I was so uncomfortable with who I was that I would finally transform into someone else.

I had completely missed how growth works. Telling myself I sucked at something wasn't making me into a better person. It just made me feel crummy. It put all the emphasis on the problem. It made me want to stay in bed and hide. It made sense in my mind to do it that way, but it didn't actually work.

When I spent time judging myself, I got better at judgment.

When I spent time hating myself, I got better at hate.

When I spent time beating myself up, I got better at that too.

I excelled at calling myself names, because I practiced all the time.

I thought I would beat myself up enough and somehow get better; I only got better at beating myself up.

I had to practice what I wanted *more* of, not what I wanted *less* of.

I had it backward. All my shame and hate had stagnated my growth rather than propelled it. Now, I was focusing on the one thing that really and truly mattered above all else: love. As I focused on love more and more and brought it into the various areas of my life, I was experiencing it more and more. I found it was more readily available for myself and for the other people in my life. I was getting familiar with what love

200

for my body looked like, sounded like, and felt like because that was what I had been studying.

Learning to love my whole self would be the same. I wasn't sure exactly what that would look like, but thanks to my time with Aphrodite, I knew I would never hate myself into self-love. The path to loving my whole self would be paved with love every inch of the way.

Self-Love takes practice.

Chapter 28

Own Your Shit

In college, there was another student who seemed just about as opposite from me as a person could get. She grew up in a larger town and was far more cultured than me. I assumed she grew up with money and was used to having money. She owned only nice things that fit and looked awesome—clearly no sale rack shopping for her. And, she was confident in her opinions. I remember hearing her talk one day about chocolate —a subject she is deeply passionate about to this day. She was saying in the most direct, matter-of-fact way, which brands she liked and which she *refused* to eat. She was so clear on what she liked and what she didn't. Never once did cost factor in to her opinion.

Growing up, my family had never been able to afford half of her preferred brands. I hadn't even tasted many of them. I only remembered eating Hershey's, and she said, "Hershey's is disgusting."

I had no idea what to do with what I heard. I was very confused seeing someone who was about my age be so confident in what they thought. I'll be honest and say it rubbed me the wrong way. Her security was such a spotlight on my insecurity. So, I did what anyone would do who didn't want to face reality. I blamed *her* for my discomfort. *She thinks she's better than me.*

Years later we reconnected. We talked every few months during all of my work with Aphrodite and I began to see her in a totally new light. Now when she clearly communicated *exactly* what she thought about parenting or fashion, I found myself experiencing *envy* rather than disdain. She was comfortable with her opinions on a level I had never personally experienced. Here was a real life person who liked who she was and wasn't trying to change and be someone else.

Kind of like Aphrodite.

I wanted to be more like that.

I went to Aphrodite with my first question: *How do I love my whole self?* I didn't get any farther than asking the question before she stopped me. She said, *"Back it up, sister, you aren't ready for that yet. You don't even know what you are trying to love."*

Touché, Aphrodite. Touché.

I was always looking for ways to be better, different. I wanted to minimize and cover up the parts of me I was ashamed of. I was constantly working to change myself.

I criticized the good.

I justified the bad.

I hid.

I fixed.

I downplayed.

I justified.

I blamed.

I avoided.

I strived.

I rationalized.

I had been doing that so much that, at this point, I wasn't even clear what the real me consisted of. I hadn't wanted to look too closely or to really see what was hidden in the dark corners of myself. I wasn't even sure what needed loving.

I couldn't love what I wouldn't even admit was there.

If I was going to make peace with myself, I first needed to figure out what I was making peace *with*. I had to become aware of every bit of me first. All the stuff I was currently working so hard to ignore. I needed to figure out who I was. And I couldn't pick and choose.

In college, one of my professors was very against replacement swear words, like saying, "Darn," instead of, "Damn." He said both words were the same because the emotion and intent behind them were the same. I started paying attention and found that I would most often say, "Dang it," or, "Shoot," after I hurt myself because I was frustrated at myself for getting hurt in the first place. I was thinking, *You're so stupid! What's wrong with you? You're such an idiot.* I was *literally* adding insult to injury, which wasn't helping anything.

What should I say if I stub my toe? (Assuming I didn't waste time beating myself up about it.) "Ouch," seemed to make the most sense. So, now when I get hurt, I say, "Ow," or, "Ouch." That's it. I'm not morally opposed to "swearing," but I don't very often—only on purpose when it is the right word to express what I want to say in the moment.

Even so, this first part of the journey to loving myself, learning *what* I was attempting to love, became for me the "Own Your

Shit" phase. I have tried to think of it in more PC terms, but I can't! ("Take ownership," "own your life," "own your stuff," or even "own your crap," just doesn't work.) When I thought of all the things that made me me—the good, the bad, and the ugly—I could only ever think of it as my "shit."

Before I could love myself, I needed to own my *shit*. All of it.

I have things I like.

I have things I don't like.

I have dreams.

I have desires.

I have a past.

I have regrets.

I have things I'm proud of.

I have things I'm embarrassed of.

I have made mistakes.

I have flaws.

I have talents.

I have shortcomings.

I have strengths.

The first step to loving myself was to take *all* these things—all my shit—out of the metaphorical bag, put them on the metaphorical table, and look at them. For this step to succeed, I would have to acknowledge that they were mine. They were real.

This process took *weeks*. I spent time just getting to know myself, asking myself questions. I asked myself what I liked, what I didn't, what I was good at, what I enjoyed about my life. I asked myself, "Why?" a lot. You might say I asked myself, "Why?" a shit-load. And I put it all on the table.

Here are some examples of "my shit."

- I like romance novels, especially ones with vampires or other supernatural creatures. My husband refuses to pick hard copies of them up from the library for me because the covers embarrass him—many have shirtless guys on them. So I only get ebook versions on my phone.

- I like to watch CW teenage dramas. It's not "prestige TV." I'm 35.

- I leave kitchen cabinets open. Often. Chris hates this.

- I don't like biographies or documentaries. Great in theory. Boring in reality.

- I like dishes—owning, not washing. If I had money to blow, and plenty of extra space, I would own at least 10 tea pots with matching cups.

- I couldn't care less about cars. I can barely recognize the models I've personally owned.

- I don't enjoy sightseeing. I'd rather explore a local market and have coffee at a cafe.

- My favorite colors for clothes are black and white. Sometimes gray.

- I am a minimalist and want all surfaces in my house clear of excess stuff. I don't do "knick-knacks" and I prefer everything to be behind closed doors. I don't even like open bookcases.

- I *love* having a vase of fresh flowers on the kitchen table. The first several years of my marriage I told my husband that I didn't like fresh flowers and not to buy me any. I *totally* lied. I just didn't think I *should* like them. I saw it as an unnecessary expense and wasteful. After realizing that I actually did like them, I had to go back and tell Chris to disregard everything I said during the first decade of our marriage regarding my stance on flowers.

All day long, I just paid attention. I paid attention to the things I looked forward to and those that I dreaded. I paid attention to what gave me energy and what drained it. I paid attention to which things I did right away and which ones I procrastinated over. I looked at what came easy to me and what was difficult. I observed strengths and weaknesses. I acknowledged areas of skill and areas where I was incompetent.

I looked at each discovery right in the metaphorical face, owned it was part of the current reality of my existence, and put it on the table. This was my shit. Big or small, dramatic or silly, positive or negative—I just looked at it and placed it in a pile. With each one I got a clearer picture of who I was and what I would be learning to love on the next leg of my journey with Aphrodite.

Self-Love begins with self-knowledge.

Chapter 29

Accept Everything

I keep my purse clean and organized, but every 6 months or so I clean it out. The last time I did this I had to question my cleanliness. The initial items I took out were things that I knew were there—sunglasses, scarf, wallet, notebook and pen, earbuds, gum—but do you know what was on the bottom of the bag? Melted chocolate. In my favorite, hand-made leather bag. I had no idea how it got there. I had no idea how long it had been there. In addition to the chocolate and customary trash bits, I found two extra ink pens, my lost chapstick, the snap to my wallet that I thought was lost, and a used plastic spoon (no doubt intentionally left in case of a dire, on-the-go, eating emergency). Lots of interesting things that I wouldn't know about if I only organized my bag as viewed from the top.

For a proper clean, you've got to empty it *all* out.

It was the same with getting all my shit out of the metaphorical bag. Lots of the initial stuff I pulled out I already knew about—my eye color, personality profiles, favorite color. I was just acknowledging it in a more direct, purposeful, and systematic way than I had in the past. Not too hard. A little uncomfortable at times, but totally doable. Some of it was new information, but mostly about things I was comfortable acknowledging—like realizing that driving in Los Angeles drained my energy (I mean, that's not a huge revelation to anyone who has driven here). Once that stuff was out, I was left with the rest—the bottom-of-the-bag grossness. It had to come out too.

I found some time when I could be alone without distractions or interruptions for what was next. I went in my room, locked the door, and sat on my bed. Pulling these last few things out of the metaphorical bag was going to be emotional and I didn't want to scare my kids if I had an ugly-cry. The final things were shoved down into the very bottom. They were dirty and grimy. They were the parts of my past that I was deeply ashamed of. So much so that I had nearly blocked them from my own awareness. I had suppressed, and repressed, and actively avoided thinking of them for years.

I wanted to leave them there.

I didn't want to take them out.

I didn't want to look at them.

I didn't want to own them as part of my story.

I didn't want them to be part of my shit.

I wanted to pretend they had never happened.

Pulling them out and placing them on the table would be messy and painful.

I also knew it was essential that I do it anyway.

I opened my notebook to a blank page and began writing down all the things from my past that I felt deep shame over— all the things I wished weren't there at all. I wrote and wrote and wrote. I filled pages with all the things I had buried in the bottom of the bag. I wrote down things that I had never said out loud to another person before. Things I had always been too ashamed to admit:

- I had multiple eating disorders.

- I had to go to a psychiatrist when I was in high school because I wouldn't stop starving myself.

- I lied right to people's faces, including people who loved me and cared for me, in order to try to cover up those eating disorders. Each instance is etched into my memory.

- In an effort to hide my purging from my family—who would meticulously watch me after meals and stand outside the bathroom door listening for retching sounds—I would vomit into empty gallon Ziplock bags in my bedroom and store them under my bed until my family was gone, then take the bags of vomit outside to the trash cans. (Just writing that makes my stomach turn. It was grotesque and born out of a desperation that breaks my heart to remember, even now.)

- I was not a virgin when I got married. The few sexual experiences I had were so wrapped in trauma, confusion, and shame that I had almost blocked them from my memory—after convincing myself that they didn't actually "count" due to various technicalities.

- In high school, when I was really depressed, I would go to weekend parties and drink until I was numb both physically and emotionally. I often drank until I vomited.

- I drove drunk a number of times, putting more than just myself at risk.

I took each of those experiences out of the bag, looked at them, placed them on the table, and owned that they were there. They existed. They really happened. And, whether I liked it or not, they were a part of my story—they were part of my shit.

I didn't celebrate them.

I didn't condone them.

I didn't make excuses for them.

I didn't try to explain them.

I didn't label.

I didn't diagnose.

I didn't place blame or try to sort out who was responsible. I honestly didn't feel like I was at that place yet. I wasn't ready to wade through them or to try to resolve them. For now, I just needed to do the work of getting them out of the bag and onto the table. I needed to acknowledge them as a real part of my past.

That was all.

As I remembered and wrote down each one, there was some intense shame that came up, but it passed quicker than I thought it would. The details of the events had faded with time, blurring at the edges, and were overlaid with all my emotions. I honestly wasn't even sure how much of my memory I could trust. I didn't try to sort through any of that. My only goal was to accept the bare facts of the situation as something that had happened.

My commitment to just acknowledge each item before placing it on the table made pulling each one out much more bearable. The hate, backlash, and self-depreciation that came after any awareness of these events had always been the worst part. I refused to do that this time.

For each item that I wrote down, I let the shame, and any other buried emotions, rise up. I was surprised to find that, perhaps more than the shame, I mostly felt sadness that they happened at all. Sadness at what I didn't know. Sadness at all the unnecessary pain.

I acknowledged that I couldn't change them now.

I couldn't imagine Aphrodite having a past like mine, since most of my actions were born out of a lack of self-love. Yet, I still imagined her in my position in order to see what she might say to herself if she were facing a list like mine.

I heard her say, *"Yes, that happened. I still love myself unconditionally. It doesn't change a thing."*

When I heard that in my mind, it was like my feet hit solid ground. My head quieted, and my heart opened. *This* was true love. Love doesn't lie. Love always tells the truth. But that truth is told from a place of unconditional love.

I had been lying to myself. I was pretending certain parts of my past weren't real, not acknowledging difficult things, even though they *were* part of my story.

I was cutting off a part of me and saying, "This part isn't worthy of love." I was looking at my past and believing it meant *I* wasn't lovable. I was using it as evidence that I was broken, bad, and not good enough. While I didn't love that these things were going on the metaphorical table, I refused to lie to myself about them anymore. I didn't want to feel ashamed when I thought about my past.

I wanted Aphrodite's love—a love that says, "I'm not going anywhere. It doesn't matter how ugly it gets, I'll be right here." I feel like that type of overwhelming love is the premise for all the great romantic love stories I flock to. It is an extraordinary love that says, "I'll never leave." I have always, *always* loved these kinds of stories. I especially love when there is some sort of supernatural element that means that the person *can't* leave, some outside regulator that means it really is forever. I always thought it made a great story, but also realized it was completely unreal. Real-life, human relationships don't work that way and, to be healthy, really *shouldn't* work that way.

Yet, I was starting to see that, while it might be unhealthy in a real-life romantic relationship to stay, "I will never leave, no matter what happens," this needed to be the foundation for the relationship with myself. That is what I needed to be able to do. I would only be able to genuinely accept everything that happened in my past if that acceptance was anchored in an unconditional, unwavering, I've-got-your-back-no-matter-what kind of love; a love that says, "I won't get scared and run. Whatever comes out of that bag, we'll face it together." *That* was the kind of love I believed Aphrodite would have for herself and I needed to channel it.

Just like with my weight, I saw that loving myself was *still* just a choice.

I chose love.

I went back through my list, read each thing I wrote down, and said to myself, *That happened, and it doesn't change anything. I love myself no matter what.*

It was draining. At the end of the time I felt thoroughly emotionally spent.

I also felt lighter.

I felt like a tightness in my chest had been released.

I felt a cleansing as the shame worked itself out.

It was, *of course*, true that those things happened. Denying and ignoring them for all these years hadn't actually kept me from feeling the pain of their reality. It had only made me feel small and weak. Owning that they did happen felt empowering. Stepping into acceptance felt like strength. Yes, this was also part of my shit and I would put it on the table along with the small and silly things. It would have a pile just like my strengths would. Big or small, it was all mine.

That day, I chose to step into my own great love story. I pledged to never leave or forsake myself. It might get bad, but I would always choose love for myself. Always.

Self-Love requires ownership.

Chapter 30

Don't Judge

Once all my metaphorical shit was on the table, I had to decide what to do with it. I knew the goal was to love myself, no matter what. I knew Aphrodite loved herself just like she was. I just couldn't *quite* grasp it. I looked at the whole table, with all my shit, and just felt a big, resounding "No" inside me when I thought of moving on from *accepting* all these parts of me to *loving* all these parts of me.

Aphrodite! This is really hard. Maybe some parts of me I could love, but not all of me. Not this pile of shortcomings over here. Not the proof right here that I'm not good enough. Not the bad stuff. Not the broken bits. Maybe some of it, but not...those.

Honestly, loving those things felt *wrong* to me.

Aren't we *supposed* to be disappointed with ourselves when we fail? Aren't we *supposed* to want to be better than we are? Aren't we *supposed* to be learning and growing? Aren't we *supposed* to be fixing the things that are wrong with us?

Acceptance felt like giving up, like settling into those things and taking residence among them. I was pretty sure that wasn't a good idea and I prepared a, *Listen here, Aphrodite,* speech in my mind. Before giving it, I decided to go back to the method.

What Would Aphrodite Do?

I imagined Aphrodite making a metaphorical pile of everything that was true about herself: strengths, weaknesses, personality traits, dreams, wants, desires, past mistakes, regrets, successes, likes, and dislikes. Then I tried to see what might be going on in her headspace.

Love was there, of course, but what I really noticed though, was what *wasn't* present. When I looked at her staring down her pile and me staring down my pile, there was one glaring thing present in my mind that wasn't present in hers—judgement.

Just like with my house, I wanted all of this shit organized! I wanted piles. I wanted clear delineations. I wanted to understand which things were good and which were bad. Which ones I was supposed to be sad about and which ones I was supposed to be proud of. I had been looking outside myself, to other people and the judgements of the world to decide what went in each pile. Yet, when I really thought about it, I didn't think I wanted to use their standards anymore. I was making more progress with love. I had been having trouble loving because I was so busy judging. I knew I needed to let go of the judgement first.

My husband broke his wrist playing high school football. He actually continued playing for almost 2 years, not knowing it was broken. When he did discover the break, it required surgery to fix. Because of the surgery, he couldn't start at the college he planned to attend where he was going to play football. All of that *seemed* bad at the time, but it led to a series of choices that landed him at the same college *I* was also attending. We met, we chose each other, and now we have an amazing marriage. I cannot imagine my life without him. We have joked multiple times that we should send a thank you card to the guy whose helmet broke his wrist!

216

I thought more about all my judging and realized that, not only was labeling everything unhelpful in most cases, I wouldn't even know for years, or maybe ever, whether something was genuinely bad or good. Something that seemed amazing, in the moment, could potentially be terrible in the long run. Conversely, some things might be good in the long run even though they were unpleasant now. And then it could all flip-flop again later on!

I am not God. I am neither all-knowing, nor all-loving. Therefore, I simply do not have the ability to accurately judge things, especially in the moment. There is so much I won't understand this side of eternity. So, I decided to step down from the position of Head Judge and give that job back to God.

I decided I didn't have to know all the answers right now, even though I wanted them. I realized I didn't have to label everything as good or bad, right or wrong—my day, traffic, the weather, other people's choices. So, I made a decision to stop. No more judging.

That didn't mean I *actually* stopped. It meant that I became aware in the act a lot. Each time I reminded myself, "I don't do that anymore," and didn't keep going down that road.

This took me to a whole new level of mental awareness where I got to really see how often I had been judging things that really weren't my place to judge. I saw how that judgement had affected my relationships—with others and with myself. I had spent ridiculous amounts of time throughout my life trying "figure it all out," judging myself, and judging other people. Looking back at my life, I could see it hadn't contributed to anything useful. It had only drawn battle lines with others and within myself.

Not judging didn't mean abdicating responsibility for my life. I didn't stop making choices that were in line with my values.

Not at all. I did move into a more peaceful space of *accepting* what was, rather than *judging* what was. I accepted my mortality and finiteness and left the judging to God. I accepted that I didn't have to know all the answers or even reach conclusions on everything.

In fact, the more I learned, the more I realized how much I didn't know. I could run myself ragged trying to find every answer, or I could accept that there was always going to be a bit of the unknown. I didn't like the unknown. I yearned for the control of clear labels. I longed for the safety that comes from having all my ducks in a row, but I was beginning to see it was an exercise in futility.

I decided there was room in my life for some mystery.

There was room in *me* for some mystery as well. I didn't always have to be able to clearly outline everything about my inner workings. I didn't have to have all the pieces in place. I didn't have to go back and figure out the context for every single emotion I experienced or choice I had made throughout my life. I didn't have to figure out who was to blame for everything that went wrong. I wanted to know myself, but I had a hunch that I would discover more with an open heart than with one hell-bent on judging and labeling.

I worked to be aware of what was true, without judging.

I thought about Aphrodite. If she were a real person, she would have liked some things more than others. She may have preferred painting to singing or one type of flower over another. She may have liked to wear particular colors. Would she have judged those likes as good or bad, right or wrong? No way! All those things were part of her, just like all of mine were part of me.

In high school, I feel like there were two distinct groups of students: the cool kids and the not cool kids. (Yes, there is more to it than that, but I'm making a point here, so follow me into the realm of sweeping generalities for the moment.) The kids who were cool, popular, and well-liked were the ones who set the trends. If they liked something, everyone else liked it too. I remember a couple of "cool kids" in my high school deciding to buy wrestling shoes and wear them around as everyday shoes. Our school didn't offer wrestling as a sport, so it had to be purely for fashion. Once I saw *those* shoes on *those* feet, I wanted a pair too. Suddenly, the idea of wearing wrestling shoes as everyday shoes seemed, not only normal, but *necessary* for happiness and wellbeing. I am certain the only reason they wore them was because they liked them. Their popularity and cool status meant they had the freedom to like whatever they wanted to like.

I realized, I had that freedom too.

I tried it on mentally first. What would it be like to not judge my shit, but to just accept it as part of me? For it to simply *be*, rather than being bad or good. If I stopped *judging* myself, I could just...*be myself.* If I removed the judgmental labels, instead of saying I am smart or stupid, strong or weak, I could just say I am...*me.* No adjectives.

I am me.

Maybe that was enough.

Maybe I could *decide* it was enough.

Maybe I could just be me without the labels.

I am me.

Self-Love follows self-acceptance.

Chapter 31

Embrace You

I recently bought a pair of quality sunglasses. Up until that day, I had never paid more than $20 for a pair. In fact, I had picked up my previous pair for $3 at a resale store. I had never even tried on a quality pair, having no intent to spend that kind of money—why get attached?

When I put this pair on, I was speechless. There is a *huge* difference between black tinted plastic and polarized, UV protecting lenses. The world genuinely *looked* different. There was contrast and vividness that I had never experienced with my $3 shades. Apparently, lenses matter.

I had been viewing all my shit through a lens smeared with a lot of judgement. I started going back through everything that was laid out on the table and applying my "no judgements" policy to each one. I went through bit by bit, pile by pile, and tried to see them with fresh eyes.

One of my dreams was to be a well-known author and speaker —someone with a message that would make a major impact on the world. I always thought that meant I was full of myself, arrogant, and self-important; but with these new lenses, I realized it was propelling me to do something with my life that would indeed make an impact on the world. It drove me to make a contribution.

I also reconsidered my harsh judgment of one of my personality profiles that said I was "controlling." That seemed awful to me—a clear flaw—even if it was true and part of my personality. However, when I put on my new lenses of self-love, I saw the truth: controlling personalities are necessary. Everyone can't be supportive. The world needs leaders to emerge.

These things had been hidden sources of shame for years, but they were transformed as soon as I was open to seeing them differently. Other piles were *much* harder to stop judging. My eyes were drawn to—what I saw as—a heaping pile of flaws stacked up at one end of the table. Things like:

- I have no sense of direction.

- I have a poor memory.

- I'm not a great dancer.

- I'm an even worse singer.

- I only speak one language.

- There are several words that, try as I might, I cannot pronounce correctly (my husband swears "Dawn" and "Don" are said differently, but I don't hear it and can't figure out how to say it like he does).

- I do not like playing My Little Ponies (or Littlest Pet Shop, or any other figure-role-playing game) with my kids.

- I sleep with my mouth open.

- I struggle to remember names.

- I have a hard time remembering dates (even my husband's birthday or our wedding anniversary).

- I struggle to put major historical events on a timeline.

These were just a few of my "flaws," a few of the things that made me feel stupid and less-than. I had to own that they were mine, yes, but what happened next? Did I have to *love* them? Acceptance was one thing, but I couldn't imagine *loving* them. It didn't even seem right.

What Would Aphrodite Do? Self-love or no, if Aphrodite were a person, she could not have been good at *everything*. *What would she do when facing down a pile of her flaws?*

As Aphrodite and I stood there looking at the table, she said, "*Who decides if they are flaws?*"

Well, that's an interesting point, Aphrodite. Who, indeed?

Who decides if something is a flaw? Who decided where the mark of "what is acceptable" lies? What is the standard that says we are falling short? Are flaws objective things that everyone agrees on? Do I *have* to see these things that way? Could I remove the label of "flaws" altogether? Is that even *allowed*?

I thought about the things I was bad at—like dancing. In truth, while some people have natural talent, being a good dancer comes from practice. It means spending time dancing. If I was spending time practicing dance, I wouldn't have that time for the things I was currently investing in—like writing this book. I would be a better dancer, but at the expense of my time, my energy, and my mental space currently going to other passions.

Being good at things requires time—unless we are in a make-believe world where I get to be the best, or even proficient, at a million activities that I never practice. The question was, did I *want* to spend time thinking about, learning about, or discussing dancing, singing, foreign language, cubism, 18th century politics, or how to play the harp? Nope. I didn't. The desire to be knowledgeable or skilled at them wouldn't have anything to do with my own wants and desires. It wouldn't have anything to do with who I was becoming. The only benefit would be to prove something to others. Or to impress them.

Aphrodite wouldn't have needed that. She already loved herself and thought she was amazing. She wouldn't have needed to quantify it or prove it. It just was.

According to Aphrodite, I could like myself *just as I was*. Even though I was still relying heavily on Aphrodite most days, I realized I didn't actually want to be a different person altogether. The crazy thing was, if I chose to fully love myself exactly as I was, then many of these things wouldn't actually be flaws. They would just be descriptors.

Just facts. Totally neutral. Simply data.

Not bad unless I decided they were bad. All the things I was currently labeling as good or bad, strength or flaw, would just be part of what made me uniquely *me*. This was just *me*.

That didn't mean I couldn't decide to learn ballet and rock it. It just meant I didn't have to be good at ballet to love myself. Being bad at dancing wasn't necessarily a "flaw" or shortcoming. It was simply something I was not currently good at. Something I had not chosen to invest enough time in to *become* good at. The funny thing is, there are plenty of things I'm not currently good at that I don't *feel* bad about at all:

- I can't fly a plane.

- I don't crochet, or knit, or quilt.

- I'm ignorant about politics.

- I can't operate a forklift.

And, I don't care! I don't even think about it. Ever! To me, *these* were just facts. They were just things I hadn't learned, hadn't tried, or tried and decided I didn't like. They were things I *chose* not to spend time on. Not doing something because I don't want to isn't a flaw, it's a choice.

Other things didn't seem to be choices at all, but rather part of how I was made. I lack spatial intelligence, which includes directions, visual-spatial estimating, and the ability to imagine things in detail in my mind. Yet, my logical-mathematical intelligence is extremely high—abstract reasoning, critical thinking, and the ability to understand underlying principles. I saw the former as a shortcoming and the latter as a strength, but is that necessarily true? What if this unique combination is for a reason? What if being wired like this is what allows me to really help people in a unique way? Like when a friend shares a problem with me, and I can easily see past the narrative and help them clearly define the underlying issue. (I have numerous examples of doing exactly that. For real. I'm good.) In those times, having a higher spatial intelligence could actually *limit* my helpfulness.

As I thought about it more, I realized it was kind of arrogant of me to look at all the things that made me *me* and assume they were flaws. I believe in a benevolent Creator, yet I had been looking at this thing He made—me—and saying it was flawed and not good enough. I was saying He did it wrong, that I should have been made different. As if my mortal brain could understand all that was at work in my creation. How rude!

Loving myself just the way I was had nothing to do with arrogance. It had everything to do with giving credit where credit was due, to the one who made me. Saying that I loved every bit of myself, just as I was, had always felt conceited to me. I realized it was the opposite. It was simply *believing* what my Creator said—that I was wonderfully made.

It was so helpful to look at all the things that were true of myself and stop labeling them as flaws and to stop thinking of myself as flawed. I didn't start labeling myself as perfect either. In light of the work I was doing with Aphrodite I had the sense that "perfect" was something that was either true of everyone or true of no one. I was grateful to not have to grapple with all of *that*. For now, I just had to know *me*.

I began stating things that were true about me in a very neutral way and working to not feel bad about those things. These days, I can say that I have to write things down or I will forget them, and not feel less-than for my memory. This is just how it is for me and I am thankful for reminders, alarms, and calendars that are integrated with my phone. Having GPS constantly running is a requirement to arrive where I'm going —it's just true. I can joyfully sing off-key and not feel ashamed of my voice.

I don't label these things as flaws anymore. I just include them in the list of things that make up the unique being that is me. I have decided to think like Aphrodite and love me just as I am. I no longer believe the lie that any of these things make me less lovable. I no longer feel the need to fix myself. I am not waiting for a future day to offer love to myself.

I spent time exploring the other piles, but once I had this lesson, it was so much easier. Self-love had nothing to do with an outside reference point. There wasn't a universal, objective level that I had to reach to love myself. If I were suddenly smarter, thinner, or possessed a new skill, it wouldn't make me more lovable. If I wasn't choosing to love myself right *now*, I wouldn't choose it *then* either.

But I *could* choose to love myself RIGHT NOW.

And I decided to.

Self-Love is available right now.

Chapter 32

Pick Your Words

Parking in LA is an adventure. One evening I had a meeting in a part of town I was unfamiliar with and was struggling to find parking. I avoid parallel parking and meters whenever I can—it's not my forte and gets expensive. I'll always choose something farther away and free and walk. I thought I had found such a spot a few blocks away from my meeting. *Perfect!* I parked and walked over. When I got back to my car at 8:20pm, there was a ticket on my windshield. It *was* okay to park there…until 8pm. Ugh.

I'm such an idiot. It says it right there! *I can't do anything right. I mean, apparently, I can't even be trusted to read. This is awful. We don't have money for this right now. This is all my fault. I hope Chris isn't mad at me. I would be mad at me. I AM mad at me. This is so embarrassing.*

I got home and burst into tears when I told my husband about the ticket. Then I spent the evening alone in my bed because I felt so small and ashamed and kept bursting into tears anytime he looked at me.

Despite the big-picture work I had done, most of the negativity in my head was directed toward the little things that happened on the regular. In these moments, my brain still jumped to unkindness first. *I'm so stupid! What is wrong with me? I have* got *to get it together.* Daily mistakes were a huge source of embarrassment, shame, and negative self talk:

- Being late because I misjudged traffic.

- Dropping things, spilling things, and breaking things, which I do a lot when I am tired.

- Accidentally sleeping in.

- Burning dinner and setting off the smoke alarm.

- Yelling at my kids because I'm tired and not managing my emotions well.

- Leaving a conversation with a friend and realizing I had talked for 80% of the time and forgot to ask them about the *one* thing I meant to ask about.

What Would Aphrodite Do? How does a woman who loves herself respond when she makes a mistake?

I took some time to check in with her. I imagined myself in the headspace of a woman who loves herself and just made a mistake. I tried to tune in to how she would speak to herself in her own mind.

"Girl, that stuff totally happens sometimes! It's over now. You've got this. You can make the best of this going forward. You can learn from this."

There was so much grace. So much love. So much patience. She spoke to herself the same way that I spoke to someone I loved when they made a mistake. And that made perfect sense. She *was* speaking to someone she loved—herself.

Face palm. *Duh!*

I had heard that so many times in church:

Love is patient.

Love is kind.

Yet, when I spoke to myself in my own mind, I was anything but.

I was impatient.

I was harsh.

I committed to practicing showing kindness to myself in the everyday moments. I knew I wouldn't change the behavior overnight, but I drew a hard line in the sand with myself and committed to not berating myself, calling myself names, or being unkind in my own mind. No more. Not for any reason. Unconditional love means no matter what, even if I break things or get parking tickets. Those are not reasons to abandon love.

It was HARD. In the moment I went right into old habits, but as soon as I saw what I was doing, I just stopped and switched my thoughts over to love.

Over.

And over.

And over again.

I kept practicing. Fortunately, I had lots and *lots* of opportunities each day. Sometimes, I didn't really know what to say, so I would imagine what I would say to someone I loved if they had just done what I had done—like my best friend. Then I spoke to myself the way I would speak to her.

Many months of practice later I was standing in my kitchen doing dishes. When I sat a newly rinsed pan on the drying mat, my elbow bumped a glass pitcher that was also drying. It bounced and rolled toward the edge of the counter. I reached for it, fingers barely brushing the smooth glass right before it went over. As I listened to the clear, high pitched crash of my pitcher shattering into a million pieces on the concrete floor, something profound happened:

I stopped.

I just *stopped.*

I took a breath and caught myself *before* I barreled down the road of unkind words. Instead, on purpose I thought, *Well, that happened! I can't change it now, but I don't have to feel bad about it. Feeling bad won't make it better. It's fine. You're okay. It was just a pitcher. You can buy a new one. Now, let's get this cleaned up and move on with more important things!*

And I did. I cleaned it up and I moved on. I felt a little sad about not having the pitcher, because I really liked it. I also felt grateful that we had enough money that I could buy a new one.

I didn't spend any time beating myself up.

I didn't call myself names.

I didn't say I was clumsy or stupid.

I chose to love myself right there, in that moment, right in the mistake. Breaking something didn't mean I was less lovable. It just meant I was human. And, once again, I realized it was *still* a choice to love.

Self-Love speaks kindly.

Chapter 33

Be Yourself

Learning to love and accept myself in my own mind was the first step to becoming Aphrodite. The next step was *acting* the way a woman who loved and accepted herself would—a woman who owned all her shit and didn't judge herself. I needed to speak and act like Aphrodite when I was around other people. I needed to stop hiding all the parts of me I had judged before.

I was invited to a Mom's event that would be the perfect time to practice. Sweet! It was a book exchange and it would be with some mamas I knew and some I didn't. During the course of the evening, someone I barely knew asked me what types of books I liked. I took a breath and tried to do what I thought Aphrodite would have done: *share honestly and openly. Don't hide. Don't put yourself down with your words.* I took a breath and told her about the book series I was currently reading and *loving*, even though I felt a little embarrassed at it —the main characters were teenagers and it was all magic and romance, a far cry from a parenting or self-improvement book which seemed to be what most people at the event were discussing.

Turns out, not only had she heard of it, she had read it—and loved it too! We got into a great discussion about all our favorite books. It was so much fun! She taught me that "vampire romance" isn't actually a genre like I thought it was. Most of what I liked fell under the genre of urban fantasy, with a few being paranormal romance. She liked that genre as well and was significantly more well-read than me. She gave me a list of must-reads. I still get all my best book recommendations from this friend and I have experienced so much joy from our ridiculously upbeat and school-girl-giddy conversations and texts about what we are reading.

Score one for living like Aphrodite.

As I shared my taste in books with more people, I discovered I actually knew multiple people who liked similar books to me, something I would never have known if I hadn't been open. I got some phenomenal novel recommendations and my reading list over the last few years would no doubt have been subpar without them.

But, deeper than that, I learned that there are people out there who will not only tolerate the parts of me that I had been hiding, but who actually like the things that I had believed made me different, other, and less-than.I also quickly learned that was not true for everyone who saw the real me.

When I was honest with another friend about what I like to read, she said, "Do you really? That surprises me," with a very (so it seemed to me) judge-y look on her face. In that moment, I wanted to retreat. Instead, I took a breath and asked myself, *What would Aphrodite do? What would she do if someone thought poorly of what she liked?*

My guess? Nothing at all.

She wouldn't have any need to defend herself, her likes or dislikes, to someone else. Their dislike wasn't a reason to go back to hiding.

I decided to pull an Aphrodite.

I simply said, "Really. And I love them!" And I left it at that.

Liking urban fantasy is just one example. I worked to show my true self to people without censoring. I tried to be more transparent and less guarded. I shared with people more about my past, especially the painful parts I had kept hidden. I said things out loud I had never said out loud before. I opened up more. I was honest more often: I said I agreed if I truly did, and I said I didn't agree if I didn't—rather than watering down my true stance to share something that I predicted they would agree with. I stopped hiding the real me. I tried to be like Aphrodite—open, honest, and in full ownership of all my shit.

My sharing was never about convincing people to believe what I believed or like what I liked. It was about me not being ashamed to share what I thought—or, in some cases, to admit I wasn't really sure *what* I thought. Sometimes, I chose to *not* share my opinion if it didn't seem appropriate. The key was that I no longer saw *myself* as something that I needed to hide.

It was stretching work. I had so much self-doubt and anxiety come up before, during, and after being open; especially when it was about something deeper than my reading list. I had to battle the old Thoughts that said the real me wasn't good enough and that I needed to present some better version of me to the world. I had spent a lot of time in my life trying to bend and shape myself into something different.

From now on, I would just be me.

Self-Love leads to authenticity.

Chapter 34

Take Compliments

I stood in my kitchen, leaning against the counter and talking to a close friend of the family. With my back against the granite and the breeze coming through the window over the sink, he gave me a very sincere and deeply kind compliment. He told me I was an amazing person and that I was going to do big things and help a lot of people with my story. I was taken aback by the profound words and *seriously* uncomfortable. I was in the process of brushing it off in my own mind, telling myself all the reasons it wasn't true, bringing out all my evidence that I had used against myself for years, running through all my normal thoughts: *That's not actually true. He's just trying to be nice. He doesn't really know me. If he did, he wouldn't say that.* I had been doing the same thing for as long as I could remember, anytime I received a compliment.

Then, I had the craziest thought: *What if he's right?*

Huh. That right there is an interesting question.

What if?

I just pondered this for a while. I considered the larger implications as well.

Maybe...maybe all the compliments I had ever received were genuine. That thought was mind blowing to me. I had simply never considered it.

I have a dear, dear friend who writes me the most loving, beautiful, words-of-affirmation filled cards on the planet—with drawings, little stickers, and doodles on both card and envelope that clearly take a significant amount of time and effort. In the past when she gave me one, part of me would feel loved, but part of me also felt guilty. I didn't believe I was lovable, so my mind told me I was a terrible person because I had tricked her into liking me. I clearly hadn't presented the real me. If I had, she would loathe me just like *I* loathed me. I was a fraud. I had hoodwinked her into thinking I was a decent person even though I wasn't. *Shame on me.*

But maybe...

Maybe her words were true. Maybe *all* those people were right —all the ones who complimented me and said kind things about me. Maybe they weren't lying or exaggerating. Maybe they weren't just trying to make me feel better. Maybe they really meant what they said and *maybe* they were right. Maybe the recognition I received from college professors was real. Maybe the unwavering belief my parents had in me wasn't dutifully faked, but genuinely felt. Maybe the people who told me I was amazing weren't actually mistaken but right. Maybe they were just saying what was true. Maybe I was more than acceptable. Maybe I *was* amazing.

That would mean the voice in my head that said I wasn't good enough was the one who was wrong. I had listened to that voice for so long without question. I simply assumed it was right. What if it had been incorrect all along? What if I, not Aphrodite, but Lorrie Gray, was good enough? Lovable? A good person? Amazing?

It was an interesting thought and one I was open to exploring. I didn't reach any conclusions that day. I wasn't ready to switch everything over just like that, but I remember concluding: *It's possible that I really am good enough. Maybe I always was. Maybe the voice is wrong. Maybe.*

Just to see, I started looking for evidence that I *was* good enough instead of looking for evidence that I wasn't. Surprisingly, I found some. Just little bits here and there, but it existed. I had simply never looked for it before.

- All the jobs I ever had came from people approaching me and asking me to work for them—I had never applied for a job.

- My kids were amazing human beings. I knew I couldn't take all the credit for that, but I reasoned I must not be doing anything *too* bad.

- My husband is amazing. I think he could have married just about anyone he wanted, but he chose *me*.

- I had friends. Amazing ones. Ones who called me to hang out when they didn't have to.

- And, at the core of all that, were God's words saying everything he had made was "good."

Some of it wasn't even *different* evidence. I was just seeing it in a different light. I used to see my perceived need to read parenting books as a sign that I wasn't a good enough parent. I told myself: *I should know this stuff already. This should come naturally. I'm failing.* Now I wondered if maybe that meant something else entirely. Maybe reading parenting books meant I was a great parent. One who was self-aware enough to see where there was room for improvement. One who cared enough to take time to learn. One who loved her kids enough to want to do right by them. What a switch! Maybe.

I made a decision that I would accept all compliments the way I had accepted all the rest of my shit. I wouldn't ever know why people said what they did, whether it was sincere or insincere, but I didn't want to outright dismiss their words either. From that day on, whenever I received a compliment, rather than immediately tossing it in the trash, I put it on the table with the rest of my shit, in the pile of compliments and kind words from others. To the person, I simply said, "Thank you," and withheld judgement regarding their motives.

It was hard.

I felt *so* undeserving of these types of compliments. I was infinitely more comfortable with a positive assessment of something I had *done*. The "doing" took time, effort, and hard work. *That* I could *earn*. But compliments where someone looked at me and simply said, "You're amazing," didn't have anything to do with what I was *doing*. It had everything to do with who I *was*. Their compliment was love shaped into words and freely offered. I was not comfortable with that. It didn't feel right to receive that kind of love without doing anything to earn it. I felt like I needed to work for it. Like it needed to hurt a little.

It didn't feel like it could just be *free*.

One glance at Aphrodite and I could see the truth.

Her love for herself wasn't earned...it was chosen. It was the unconditional and no-matter-what kind of love. The same would be true when offering unconditional love to another person—it could never be earned, because there weren't any conditions to meet. Someone could simply *choose* to love me.

Alternately, I could also simply *choose* to love them.

I made the decision; I would never turn away love. Unconditional or not, I knew I wanted more love in my life, so

I would freely accept what was freely offered. It would all go on the table.

I would strive to give the same type of unconditional love to the people around me, based on nothing more than my choice to love them.

And above all, I would continue to freely offer love to myself.

Self-Love is free.

Chapter 35

Take Care

I was chatting with a friend one day and she talked about scheduling a massage because she needed to do some self-care. I had been thinking a lot about *self-love*, but hadn't really considered *self-care* or how it fit in with what I was doing.

To me, self-care was comprised of getting a massage, getting a mani/pedi, or taking a bubble bath. I could only afford the first two on rare special occasions and the third never worked out the way I hoped. Sitting in the tub was uncomfortable, part of me was always cold, my arms got tired holding my book up, and I was always afraid of getting the book wet.

I did some reading and Googling and discovered that self-care is much broader than I originally thought. It includes all the ways we care for ourselves in every area of our lives: physical, mental, emotional, spiritual, social, and vocational. When I thought of all the things I was learning to do to show love for myself, I realized many qualified as self-care. I was so excited to realize I had actually been doing self-care this whole time and didn't know it!

I started looking for all the little ways I was caring for myself already: I drank enough water each day; I took quality supplements; I went to bed at a reasonable hour; I stretched and moved my body; I ate nourishing food.

I realized that all the ways I was no longer hurting myself also counted as self-care. I care for myself by abstaining from harmful things. I care for myself when I don't eat to manage my emotions. I care for myself when I don't overeat. I care for myself when I abstain from sugar.

I had been loving myself really well in areas directly related to my physical body, and my thoughts were much kinder (which was definitely a way to care for myself mentally and emotionally), but I realized that I could also show more love and care to myself in the other areas. I spent time brainstorming ideas and adding in more self-care to my day.

Not to brag, but I'm pretty great at this now. Not all of it looks like what I thought of as self-care, but it is all part of how I take great care of myself, so I count it. A lot of my list takes little or no extra time, so I actually do it!

- I listen to music.
- I buy myself flowers.
- I spend time lying in the sun.
- I say no when I mean no.
- I take breaks.
- I got a standing desk.
- I got rid of pants that cut off my circulation.
- I stop work at dinner time.
- I intentionally take deep breaths throughout the day.
- I buy high-quality food.

It is all motivated by love. Just like with self-love, I think true self-care is less about *what* we do and more about *how* we do it. Everyday actions can be transformed into acts of self-care if we are doing it for the purpose of loving and caring for ourselves.

And it doesn't have to be big or take a lot of time. My beauty routine used to be something done out of hate (definitely not self-care). Now it was truly an act of self-love because I was appreciating my body through the whole process. I realized it *also* qualified as self-care.

I care about myself, so I show it. I think that is the key. Rather than trying to *do* self-care, I think we need to genuinely *feel* love, which will naturally lead to caring for ourselves. The doing follows the feeling. If you love your body, you will care for your body. If you love yourself, you will care for yourself.

These days, the two concepts are so entwined in my mind I often don't even distinguish between them and use the words interchangeably. I think of it this way: Self-love is something we *feel* and self-care is something we *do*. Self-love is always what drives true self-care. I don't believe you can truly love something and not care for it. One necessitates the other.

Self-care that isn't driven by love is often driven by obligation and guilt and it becomes one more task.

One more outside expectation to meet.

One more thing we *should* be doing.

The biggest reason most women say they can't do self-care, and one of the reasons I used to give as well, was believing I didn't have time. My general thoughts about time were that I didn't have enough, I was behind, and I needed to hurry up. That was my story and I believed it wholeheartedly. This narrative did not create an environment conducive to taking time for self-care.

What Would Aphrodite Do? What would her story be about the time available to her?

I think she would have *made* time. Period. If her body was her most valuable asset, then caring for it came first. She would

240

never have ignored its signals and risked damaging it for something as mundane as a clean house. Caring for her body would have been her number one priority. A clean house wouldn't have even been a close second. It might have squeaked in around 50th place. And she loved *herself* too, which included her mind and emotions. I think she absolutely would have made time to care for those things.

The truth? She and I would have the same 24 hours, just like every other person on the planet. We were just choosing to spend them differently. She would make time for herself. For years I hadn't. Why?

Simple. All that time, I hadn't viewed myself as valuable and worthy enough to care for. Every other thing in my day seemed more important. I saw my needs as a lower priority than the needs of others. Aphrodite would not have. Loving herself was not about short-changing others or letting them down. Rather, loving herself was about counting her needs as *equal* to the needs of others.

To live like Aphrodite, my needs would be prioritized and matter to me *as much* as the needs of my family and my community. I would still serve and make sacrifices for those I loved, but I would also extend that service and sacrifice to myself in equal measure. I would acknowledge that I mattered. Taking time to care for myself in this way would give me the required energy to serve others well.

A regular self-care routine flowed naturally once I decided I was worth the time. The truth was, the time had always been there. Same 24 hours as everyone else. Now I knew I was worth taking time for.

Self-Love results in self-care.

Part 5: Becoming Aphrodite

Chapter 36

On and On We Go

My work with Aphrodite was never complete, but simply took on different forms. The love I learned from her flowed like a gentle river into all the little crevices and cracks in my life that needed to be filled with love. I didn't have any other goals or agendas at this point, I just wanted more of this thing I had. I had already surpassed anything I had ever imagined was possible.

One day I did a session with Aphrodite to see what opportunities for love I might have missed in my day. I imagined Aphrodite waking up in the morning. What would she do first? I imagined her stretching her body, a first act of love. Yet, even though that was loving for her body, I imagined that her thoughts wouldn't have been about her body at all. She was secure in her body's beauty. I thought her mind would have been full of positive thoughts about the upcoming day; about all the amazing things she would do while living in a body she loved.

Before my work with Aphrodite, I had a different habit. First thing in the morning, as soon as I was conscious, I put my hand on my stomach, felt my belly fat, and pinched it between my thumb and forefinger to "measure" it. Every. Single. Morning. I don't know when this started or why, but there was always fat there, always something to pinch—especially due to the loose skin that comes from 2 pregnancies. That meant I started every day thinking about how fat, ugly, and disgusting my body was. And, you know what? That thinking tends to create a crummy start to the day. My first thought about myself was how much I wanted to change my body. That mood carried into the rest of the day. Even after my initial work with Aphrodite, I still kept this habit. While I didn't call myself names anymore, the practice still created a tinge of sadness and disappointment, a slight frustration that regardless of what I did to nourish and care for my body I could always pinch an inch.

I decided to put a stop to the morning belly fat check. Unlike the scale, which I had redeemed for love, I realized I didn't really need or want to redeem this. I would know if there were major changes in my body composition that required my attention if my pants started to fit differently. I simply could not see a woman who was convinced of her body's beauty doing this.

The first morning I chose *not* to do this, I felt so off balance, not sure what to do with myself instead. I couldn't just remove this habit without adding something to fill that void. As I lay in bed, rather than checking my belly fat, I checked in with myself. I took a minute to pay attention to how I was feeling—physically, mentally, emotionally. I thought about my upcoming day and imagined myself walking through it with love. I put my feet on the floor and I told myself, "*Today is going to be amazing.*"

It wasn't a lot of words. It wasn't a flowery speech about awakening my inner goddess, but I made it a point to think this, on purpose, first thing in the morning. Sometimes I followed it up with a little more if no one immediately needed my attention: *Today is going to be amazing. I've got this. I can handle what comes my way. Everything will work out. It will all be*

245

fine. I love my life. Or whatever else came to mind. Just basic positive thinking.

The words may have been few, but it really made a difference. I had been starting each day in an emotionally negative spot, which made it hard to deal with the things that came my way —and with kids, there tends to be a lot that comes one's way in the morning. This little pep talk in the mornings put me in a positive mindset and I found myself more able to handle the morning chaos with a better attitude.

I could keep going on and on about my process indefinitely, but here's the summary: I applied my WWAD method to every area of my life, overhauling old mindsets and habits bit by bit and piece by piece. I just kept asking, *What else? What's next? What Would Aphrodite Do Here? And here? And* here*?* Season by season new areas were uncovered that needed love. I invited Aphrodite in to transform it all.

- I grew in my relationships. As I learned to show love to myself, I found that I no longer had an aching need for others to do it for me. I was less needy with people and put fewer demands on them.

- I learned to set boundaries, because boundaries are loving and keep us safe.

- I began parenting like a mother who loves not only their kids, but herself as well. (Game changer, my friends.)

- I looked at my dreams and decided, *I love myself enough to pursue these.*

- I set goals for myself, even though it was uncomfortable. (Discomfort can actually be loving.)

- I created breathing room in my schedule.

- I let other people be wrong about me. (And I loved them anyway.)
- I quit activities and committees that I didn't want to do anymore.
- I stopped cooking so much.
- I spent money investing in myself.

I rejected normal and conventional in favor of radical self-love.

I Aphroditied it all. And I have no plans to stop.

Chapter 37

She is Me

Nearly a year and a half after I initially started my WWAD process, I got a bit of a shock. I woke up truly excited to start the day. I really believed it would be a good one. I didn't have to *tell* myself to think that. I was just genuinely excited about the life I had crafted...and that excitement had *nothing* to do with my weight or what I would be eating that day. I didn't even think about pinching my belly fat. I was excited about my actual life, something that was no longer intertwined with my food intake.

When I got hungry, I didn't have to try to generate feelings of calm; I simply wasn't freaked out anymore. It was no longer scary. I didn't have to persuade myself to eat nourishing food or take care of my body, it just felt right to do so; I *wanted* to care for it. I wasn't actively trying to think loving thoughts about myself or my body to override the mean, negative thinking; kind thoughts *flowed naturally*. When I stopped to think about it, I realized the old Thoughts just weren't there very often.

I went through the entire day, got to the end of it, and realized I had not needed to visualize Aphrodite at all. I hadn't taken time to actively think loving thoughts. I hadn't needed to ask her for wisdom. I hadn't needed to watch her to know what the loving thing to do was.

I was doing all those things already.

I knew the answers.

I was thinking loving thoughts automatically.

I was acting in loving ways on my own.

When I thought about myself and my body, for the first time I was genuinely *feeling* love. I felt warmth. Kindness. Compassion. Camaraderie.

I wasn't pretending anymore. I wasn't faking it. I actually *felt* love. Not as someone imitating a woman loving herself, not through Aphrodite's headspace, but as *me*.

I, Lorrie Gray, loved myself.

When did this happen? Is this for real?

I went to the mirror to test it out.

I looked at my body in the mirror, really looked at it, and said, *I love this body just as it is,* and I realized I really did. Rather than cataloging flaws, my brain told me all the reasons *why* I loved this body: *This is my body. I'm so grateful for it. It lets me hug my girls. It carried my babies. It has two functioning legs. It is a wonder. It's mine and I like it.*

I did not have blinders on. I didn't suddenly believe that my body was "perfect" and I would suddenly have people beating down my door to pose on the cover of magazines in a bikini. I wasn't convinced I was the most beautiful woman in the world. It was still my body. I still had a disability, I still had pain, I still had stretch marks and cellulite. But I loved it. Because it was mine. It was the only one I would ever have and I *wanted* to care for it and treat it with kindness. I *wanted* to love it. So I did.

I looked myself right in the eye and said out loud, "I love and accept myself," and realized it was true. I wasn't faking. I really *did* love and accept myself. All of myself. All my shit. Everything from my past. This was me and I didn't want to be anyone else.

I wasn't saying *I* was perfect either. I didn't believe I was suddenly the one person who would never make an error. I wasn't immune to losing my temper or being insensitive. I just didn't believe I had to be someone different to love myself. I loved who I was. And I loved the person I was becoming.

I had finally learned in my heart, not just in my head, Aphrodite's main lesson for me, the one that ran through everything else:

Unconditional Love means love without any conditions whatsoever.

It means no matter what.

It means it isn't earned.

It is unqualified,

unreserved,

unwavering,

wholehearted,

unlimited,

complete,

total,

full,

and without any restrictions.

I didn't love myself because I had fixed everything about myself that was wrong. I just finally knew that I didn't need to. Unconditional love was always freely given, and I had finally allowed myself to give it to myself with no strings attached. I simply loved myself. That was all. I didn't have to justify it or back it up with logical reasons why I deserved it now. My only real reason was that I wanted to. I chose to.

I couldn't pinpoint the day or the hour it happened. I probably couldn't even get close. But somehow, somewhere along the journey of trying to imitate Aphrodite, the pretending had become real. What started out as an exercise in faking it had become a truth. My truth.

I did love myself. I really did. I was equal parts shocked and overjoyed to discover it. I had been aiming for tolerance, daring to hope for acceptance, and I ended up with genuine, unconditional self-love.

How about that?

That wasn't the end of the road though. I still had negative thoughts about my body sometimes; I still occasionally looked in the mirror or caught my reflection in a store window and thought: *I look fat today*. I sometimes thought it would be better if I was a little different: *I talk too much. I'm not smart enough.* The difference now was those thoughts did not feel completely true anymore, they felt like I was thinking them out of habit. They felt like a lie. Now, love and acceptance felt more natural and more true than the hate. It was so strange. Originally, saying I loved myself felt foreign, and the hateful thoughts felt familiar, but at some point they had flip-flopped. Even so, for a time, I lived with both. When the negatives ones popped up, I just continued directing my mind to Aphrodite-like thoughts. Correction: to Lorrie-like thoughts.

At the 2 year mark, I was in bed one night, trying to fall asleep. Like so many evenings, I found myself praying. Nothing formal, just a casual conversation with some thanksgiving mixed in. As I was telling God what I was grateful for, I prayed, "Thank you for making me just like you did. Thanks for making me, *me*," and nearly fell out of bed! Did I really just pray that? Did I really just think that? I had never *ever* thought or prayed that before. Every prayer where I was mentioned had been for God to forgive me, change me, help me, grow me, make me better. Lying there that night, I thought about me— all of me—and I just felt thankful. Maybe He knew what he was doing all along.

I was seeing everything so differently now. The choice to love and accept all of myself was opening up entirely new ways of seeing myself. It was like my eyes were open to who I really was for the first time. I used to look at myself and see so many things that were wrong with me, but now I was starting to see how many things were right.

I didn't take credit for the parts I had no control over, because that credit belongs to the God who made me. However, I also decided it was okay to feel proud of myself for the things I had controlled. I made the choices. I did the work. I persisted. I leaned in when it got hard, rather than pulling back. I took the mind He made and used my free will to direct it to love. And I felt gratitude and appreciation for the choices I had made.

I was so surprised by all of this genuine self-love. It took me a long time to really wrap my mind around it. It was weird to be able to tell people that I loved myself and say it as *me*—not me imitating Aphrodite. I really wanted to figure out how in the world this happened. It wasn't part of the plan and I was more than a little confused. Thankful? Yes. But also confused. *How did I end up actually loving myself?*

I found some time to curl up on my comfy couch. I brought water and tea, a notebook, and a pen, fully prepared for a long session of sorting it out. I tucked my knees up under me and settled in. I took a breath and asked, *How did this happen?*

The preparation for a long session was unnecessary.

As soon as I asked, the answer came.

It floated to me like a calm breeze:

She was never real.

Right.

There never *was* an Aphrodite.

It was never *her* wisdom that guided me; it had always been my own.

It wasn't *her* thoughts in my mind showing me how to love myself; they were my own.

She didn't actually exist in my visions; they were all constructed by me from my own understanding of what love looks like.

She wasn't speaking to me; I was speaking to me.

She wasn't showing me anything; I was showing me everything.

She wasn't real; I was real.

Everything I needed had always existed inside of me, but I had not been allowing myself to access it. I had always known *how* to love myself. I simply hadn't thought I *deserved* to. I believed if I showed myself undeserved and unearned love the universe would strike me down for it. I believed so strongly that I was not deserving of that kind of love, and I had so much evidence to prove it, that I couldn't see anything else. I wouldn't *let* myself see anything else. I was too busy with my own hate. There was no space left for love.

Each day that I acted in loving and kind ways towards myself, each day that I thought kind thoughts and said kind words, I was building up evidence for the opposite. I was proving that I was lovable with each act of love. With every kind word I showed that I deserved kindness. Every time I took care of myself I proved I was valuable and worthy of care. And each time that no one called me out on it, each time there was no lightning strike from the heavens, each time there was no intervention from God saying this wasn't for me, I began to believe it a little more. I had been actively loving myself for the last two years, so I had a lot of evidence that I was, in fact, lovable.

I wonder if, perhaps, we are actually hardwired for love from birth. If maybe we don't begin to hate until we are taught to. My time with Aphrodite was a remembering. It was a coming home. Aphrodite was the key I needed to unlock what had been there all the time: a woman who truly loved herself, just as she was.

I now know that being "lovable" doesn't have anything to do with the one being loved. It has everything to do with the one who is doing the loving. It is about whether they are *able* to love—love-able. Aphrodite showed me that I *was* able to love myself. I knew how. I just had to choose it.

I am able to love myself.

I am lovable.

I am deserving of love.

Chapter 38

Changing the Question

Realizing that I did truly love myself, and that it was *me* doing the loving and teaching all along took this work to the next level. My ultimate goal was still to live like someone who loves herself—and to learn more and more what that meant. The only real shift was that now I asked, *What is loving?* rather than *What Would Aphrodite Do?*

Three and a half years later, it is still a process. Unloving thoughts still pop up from time to time, but they don't trouble me. They are remnants of a past life, habitual, knee-jerk reactions and nothing more. I am focused on who I am becoming. I am loving myself everyday in a perfectly imperfect way, and that is enough.

Anytime I need it, anytime I'm struggling to love, I spend time checking in with the goddess who is me, i.e., the woman who loves and accepts herself fully. I access the part of me that already knows how to love myself well, and I bring it to the front. I direct my mind toward loving thoughts and I walk out that love regardless of what else is happening in my life. And while I don't always *feel* love, I always believe that I am lovable—that I am deserving of receiving love and that I am able to give it to myself.

I always believed that other people were valuable and worthy of love and care, I just put myself in a different category. They didn't have to earn it, but I did. Examining my own mind had uncovered so many mindsets that really didn't make any sense when I thought about it rationally. If it was true for the rest of the planet, then it was true for me. I wasn't the one, single exception in the entire history of time. I deserved love, kindness, forgiveness, rest, and good things as much as the next person. Not more, not less, but *as much as.*

Even so, sometimes, I still struggle. Sometimes, I simply can't seem to access that part of me that knows how to love myself. When that happens, I go back to Aphrodite as my reference point (even though I know she is really just me). I get out of my own head and imagine Aphrodite. I imagine a woman who loves herself and isn't entangled in my story. I use her to help get a concrete picture of a woman who fully loves herself. I ask what *she* would do and think and feel in my situation, then I do that.

It can feel a little awkward, maybe even a little forced at times, but deep down I know what I believe about myself. I don't toss it all out because I'm having a bad day or hormonal. I don't abandon my belief in my lovability in favor of whatever thought pops into my head in the moment. I trust what I know in my bones:

I love myself.

Not because I never have an unloving thought enter my mind.

I am a woman who loves herself because that is who I choose to be.

Chapter 39

And I Danced

Shortly after beginning my work with Aphrodite, a couple friends and I started an informal mastermind group. We met once a month to share about what was going on in our lives, offer support and advice to each other, and clarify our intentions for the next month. It was *so* refreshing and helpful in a season when I had so much going on. We typically met at coffee shops or cute cafes around Los Angeles. One week in particular will stick with me for the rest of my life. I had just finished my turn of sharing. I don't remember what I said, but my friend's response was, "You should dance naked."

Say what?

My other friend piped up, "Ooooh! Yes. Naked dancing would be *so* great for you."

I had a number of followup questions, both practical and cognitive to said suggestion. I loved these two ladies, but was a tad confused as to how the conversation had taken *that* turn. I didn't dance. I didn't spend much time naked. I could not fathom doing them at the same time. The visions in my head of the undulating flesh was not something I felt excited to act out in real life. Politely, I thanked them for the suggestion, promised to consider it, and kept that little nugget in the back of my mind.

After beginning my work with Aphrodite, I began to understand what my friends had seen so clearly—I was seriously repressed on a lot of levels. Now it finally felt like something I could explore. I waited until I was home alone, worked up some courage, went in the bathroom, locked the door (just in case), and took off my clothes. I had a solid minute or two of wondering, *now what? Do I need music? Does the style of dance matter?* I tried out a few initial awkward movements that were closer in resemblance to a cheer routine. Then, I closed my eyes and just moved. It may not have qualified as "dancing" by anyone else's standards, but I did eventually find a space where movement and feeling seemed to intertwine into something *more*. Something deep. Something with soul.

It was a very interesting experience. It is *not* an experience that I have felt the need to repeat regularly, but I did find a lot of freedom that day. I consider naked dancing decidedly advanced WWAD work, and, although I didn't pass with flying colors, I do think I passed. It is a tool I now pull out if I need to act out in the physical realm what I believe: there is freedom in total self-love.

I also did some plain ol' (clothed) dancing in my regular life. As a young girl, I danced more, but I hadn't moved my body in those kinds of ways since my disability. Physically, I had to be careful, but I realized that dancing was perhaps the very definition of joyful movement. So, I started playing music during the day and dancing with my kids. I danced alone in my kitchen when I felt like it. Sometimes to a song. Sometimes just a random, totally uncoordinated ballerina twirl simply because I felt like it. I wasn't planning to take up lessons, I just wanted to move my body for fun, when I felt like it, in the moment, regardless of what anyone else thought about it. So I did. I still do. And as I learned to love myself more and more, there were simply more times when there was a joy that bubbled up and *begged* to be let out via some ridiculous dance moves.

Even more than the actual dancing—or the actual naked dancing—the metaphorical concept of dancing naked became my heart song. For me, it represented not only sharing openly who I was, but doing it with the confidence that comes from an unwavering love for oneself. Up until this point I would sometimes bare part of my metaphorical nakedness to people —choosing to be open and honest—but I always wanted to cover up right after. Basically, I was naked, but I wasn't comfortable with it. The idea of being naked and going so far as to dance in that nakedness was a freedom I had never even glimpsed until now.

"Dance Naked" became a mantra for me. A call to live a life that was bravely me. It went beyond not hiding my opinions, likes, dislikes, talents, and weaknesses (let alone body). Dancing naked meant stepping into true freedom and joyfully celebrating the things I wanted to hide before.

This was uncomfortable and uncharted territory. I'm thankful for the complete works of Brené Brown (if you haven't seen her break-out TED Talk, stop reading this and Google it) and other incredibly insightful humans that taught and inspired me on my journey toward dancing naked, which started with the ability to just stand there naked and vulnerable, long before any dancing really occurred. It took time. It is still often a conscious choice. But it got easier with time.

I was seeing vulnerability with new eyes now. Previously, the biggest fear had always been that I would open up to someone and then be rejected. I realized now that the absolute worst part was not actually their rejection—though that was bad—it was my rejection of myself. The truly awful part was me believing I didn't deserve wholehearted acceptance. If someone said something even marginally unkind, I would take it on and make it the gospel truth. I would beat myself up. I would use it against myself. I would tell myself I wasn't good enough. I would feed the shame and self-loathing for days. I would carry their words around within me and experience that pain over and over again, each time I replayed it.

Winston Churchill said, "When you're 20, you care what everyone thinks. When you're 40, you stop caring what everyone thinks. When you're 60, you realize no one was ever thinking of you in the first place." I actually knew lots of women who fit the 40's part of this quote. It seemed that at a certain point these women just flipped the world the metaphorical bird. They were unapologetically themselves—which is great. However, when I compared it to the Aphrodite I saw in my mind's eye, it was very different. These women said, "This is just who I am," in a challenge-me-if-you-dare kind of way. Like, if you didn't like them, they might give you a piece of their mind for it, or at the very least, stomp off in a huff of righteous indignation. Aphrodite said, *"This is who I am"* with a quiet, confident, grounded assurance born of genuine self-acceptance.

I decided I wanted to jump directly to the 60's part. I figured most people were probably like me, spending lots of time stuck in their own heads. They might judge me for a minute, but then they would pretty quickly go back to thinking about...themselves.

What is loving?

I couldn't control other people or their opinions of me, but I could control myself. I could decide if I let one person's words shatter everything I had come to believe or if I let it remain simply one person's opinion. I could internalize it or I could hand it right back to them and let them keep it. I didn't have to be hurt and offended just because they shared their thoughts. Humans have every right to do that.

Even if someone actively tried to hurt me with their words, I still wasn't powerless. I always got to decide what I thought about their words. I got to decide what I thought about the other person for saying them. I got to decide what I thought about me, even if the awful things said about me were *true*. Regardless of their choices, I could always choose love for *both* parties.

Sometimes, love might look like a truly grateful, "Thank you for telling me!" Sometimes, it might be a, "Thanks for your opinion, I'll think more about that." And sometimes it might look like walking away. It never looked like self-loathing or revoking love for myself. It never looked like playing the victim. It never looked like blaming others for what I chose to do with their words.

While I would love to receive love, acceptance, and kindness from every single person I encounter for the rest of my life—especially everyone I share the deep and painful things with—I know it won't happen. I also know it isn't necessary. I don't have to wait to see what someone else decides to think about me to figure out if I'm good enough. I don't need an outside reference point to practice unconditional love for myself.

I decided that, no matter what happens and no matter what others say or do, I would always show love, acceptance, kindness, and compassion to myself. With that decision made, I took up permanent residence in the realm of radical self-love. And I found I was finally free to dance—naked.

It still took courage sometimes, but not as often. I found I simply wasn't as afraid as I had been. The greatest danger had always come from myself, and now, that danger was gone. I knew I could rely on myself and that gave me a confidence I didn't have before. I wouldn't be able to predict what others thought of me, but I could always control what I thought of me. That was more than enough.

For the first time in my life, I found I could take criticism and it not be a crushing experience. I used to *hate* criticism. Even the smallest suggestion from my husband was met with a 5-minute explanation. I would present an elaborate case to show why I didn't need to change. Given enough time to postulate, I could even find a way to make the entire situation his fault. Accepting I had done something imperfectly meant entering the realm of self-loathing. So, I found ways to justify my actions or place blame elsewhere. I'm not proud of this, but there it is. *Out of the bag and on the table.* Now I knew unconditional love didn't come from anything I did, but was a choice I made. When I committed to loving myself no matter what, I could actually hear the other person and weigh their words. I still don't particularly *enjoy* receiving criticism. But I do love when, after receiving it, I tell myself, *This doesn't change a thing. I love you no matter what.*

I became a safe place for my own soul.

And within the safety of my own self-love,

I danced.

Chapter 40

This is Me

I had come really far with self acceptance, self love, openness, vulnerability, and dancing naked in my own life. I was finally comfortable with myself and liked the woman I saw in the mirror.

Even so, I had not shared the new, more confident, more loving version of me beyond my inner circle, those I already knew loved and accepted me too. I had been holding back from putting myself into the greater world and sharing my story on a larger scale.

Truly loving and accepting myself meant not hiding myself from *anyone*.

Before my work with Aphrodite, I held back, believing I wasn't really good enough to make a genuine contribution. Now I knew I was just as valuable as the next person, and, beyond that, I had learned some stuff that people might also want to learn. It was time to start speaking out. Letting my voice be heard. For me, genuine, unwavering self-love meant no longer holding myself back, but bravely putting myself into the world and letting myself be seen. It meant sharing my story.

Sometimes, I found myself afraid of the failure and the mistakes. I found I was often terrified to share anything, since I clearly didn't know everything. I wasn't an expert or a researcher. I could totally screw this whole thing up. That was scary and a lot of pressure.

Yet, I found I was perhaps *more* terrified and overwhelmed by the possibility that I might be truly amazing. I didn't even know what to do with a thought like that. I always had this sense that there was something amazing inside me, a gift of great worth. Yet, I didn't think I *should* feel those things, so I played small. It felt prideful and vain to think I could help; to think I was worthy of an amazing life; to think my story might connect with people on a larger scale. All those excuses were gone now. I knew that was true for me as much as the next person. I knew I was good enough. I knew I was valuable. It was time to start acting like it.

I had not posted on social media for 3 years. Of course, no one *needs* to post on social media, but it was something I used to do and then stopped. I stopped because my self-loathing was so great that posting anything that was even remotely positive felt like a lie. I didn't like myself. I was embarrassed to show "me" to the world. I was absolutely certain that they wouldn't like me either. That they would judge me. I would write posts and delete them. I would consider it and then back out.

I thought back over all that I had learned:

I had been in a wheelchair and now I wasn't!

I had learned to love my body.

I had learned to love myself.

I learned to not beat myself up.

I learned to lose weight from a place of love and kindness.

I loved my life.

I was becoming the woman I had always wanted to be.

I knew without a shadow of a doubt that others could benefit from my story, and I was the only one who could share it. I *knew* I was strong enough. My unwavering commitment to love and accept myself made me strong enough. So…

- I made my first Facebook post.

- I *finally* accessed the Instagram account my husband had created for me a year before.

- I launched a life coaching business.

- I created a website.

- I got my first set of headshots.

- I made videos of myself talking about what I learned about self-care and posted them.

- I took my very first selfie at age 34 and posted it.

- I did a live video that was open to the entire world.

It wasn't all smooth sailing, not by a long shot. The first time I tried to get photos of myself for my website, none of them were usable because I looked like I was in pain in every one—I was…emotional pain! The first time I tried to record a video for my website, I did multiple takes over the course of a couple of hours and had to scrap the whole thing. Even after all the work I had done for myself, putting myself out to the larger world brought up so much self-doubt.

Around this time, I saw a preview for an upcoming film called The Greatest Showman. As I watched and listened I heard these song lyrics, "I am brave. I am bruised. This is who I am meant to be. This is me." At that moment, when I first heard Keala Settle belt *"This is me,"* I felt such a strong resounding *yes* in my spirit. It spoke to me exactly where I was at. I connected with the song long before I watched the film. It put to rhythm so many of the lessons I had been learning—that I could accept me just like I was. All my shit, all the parts of me, they all made me *me*.

Perhaps I was the person to share this story *because* of my bruises rather than in spite of them.

As I was considering sharing my story with the world, I knew the painful parts were the most impactful. People didn't want to hear what I had learned until they knew where I had been. They connected with the parts where I still felt a little bruised. The parts that took bravery to share. "This is me," became my anthem as I put myself into the world.

I am brave. I am bruised. This is who I'm meant to be. This is me.

I started playing the song before I got photos taken. I played it before I needed to record a video. I played it when I thought the anxiety would crush me after posting something on social media. I played it when I made public mistakes. I played it when I lacked the courage I needed. I listened over and over and sang along until I *knew* that I was exactly who I was meant to be, bruises and all; until I remembered that those bruises were *why I had something to share*. When I got to the place where I felt the urge to stomp my foot, throw my arms wide, and declare, "This is me!" *then* I went and did what I needed to do.

With this as the soundtrack of my days, I let more and more people see me, knowing full well that many of them would not love me. Many would not accept me. Many would not connect with my message. Many would judge me. Just as before, like a pair of pants that didn't fit quite right, it wouldn't mean something was wrong with me. If someone didn't like me, that would be about them—what they liked or didn't. No need to blame anyone. That is just how it goes. People get to have opinions. They get to like what they like and dislike what they dislike. I didn't need anyone else to like me for *me* to like me.

Learning to love the photos themselves was a whole additional level of advanced work in self-love, and it took time. Not surprisingly, I learned I could think and feel love about photos if I wanted to. Even about photos with bad angles. A crummy photo was not a reason to abandon unconditional self-love and slide into negative self-talk. I wanted to love me—regardless. That meant working to think loving thoughts about *all* the photos. Every. Single. One. When I see photos of myself, even if my eyes are closed or I have a double chin, I still think, *Hey, I like her*, just before I hit delete.

I noticed an interesting bonus effect of this work. Even though my anthem was all about "me" and my focus was on putting myself and my face out into the world, it actually helped me become *less* inwardly focused. Letting myself be seen really required me to stop making my interactions with others so much about myself. I had to get over the idea of everyone liking me. I had to learn to manage my own emotional life.

When I stopped thinking so much about whether or not people like me, or what they thought of the size of my stomach, I found that I showed up differently in my life. I showed up differently for my friends as well. As a woman who loved and accepted herself, I didn't need to prove anything. I didn't need anyone else's love, though I cherished it when it was freely given. I found I was able to be more present in conversations, more focused on others. I was able to think outside of whether or not the world would like me and explore how I could serve the world *as* me.

Before Aphrodite, I spent so much of my time trying to figure out who I was and who I was supposed to be. I thought I was looking for something "out there." I was always waiting to arrive. Now, for the first time, I felt like I was right where I was supposed to be.

The destination wasn't about where I was going. It was always about who I was becoming.

I *am* who I'm meant to be.

This is me: A woman who loves and accepts herself.

A real-life, modern-day Aphrodite.

Conclusion

Why it Worked

I genuinely had no idea what I was doing when I started this journey with Aphrodite. None at all. I'm not even sure you could say there was a definite start. It's a miracle of epic proportions any of this worked. After all, the whole process was based on nothing but a four-word question born out of a last-ditch attempt at survival. I didn't tell anyone about my journey for a long time. I shared some of the lessons, but left out Aphrodite.

As I read more self-development books, watched films about the body image movement, watched training videos from life coaches, and connected with all-around amazingly smart people, I began to finally, retroactively, make sense of why this method was so incredibly effective, albeit atypical. Looking back, it makes perfect sense.

1. Visualization

There is power in seeing what we want in our mind before we go do it. One of the keys to effective visualization is to try to make what you want as real in your mind as possible. This was what I was doing when I pictured Aphrodite. I imagined her thoughts, her feelings, her actions. Even though I wasn't imagining *me* there, I still benefited from the imagining. In those sessions I was showing my brain what to think and feel in various situations. I had already "seen" myself acting in loving ways in my own mind. Then, when I did it in real life, it felt more natural. I had created new, loving neural pathways and then I simply strengthened them through repetition.

2. Thought Work

I have been impacted tremendously by the teachings of Brooke Castillo. She is the creator of the Self-Coaching Model (shown below). This Model presents a number of self-help concepts in easy to understand and easy to apply language.

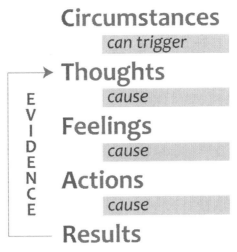

Reprinted with permission from the author
Brooke Castillo (www.brookecastillo.com).

Brooke will tell you that she didn't invent the concepts shown, but learned them from other teachers like Byron Katie, Abraham Maslow, Tony Robbins, and Martha Beck. This is just the way the world works. She took their teachings and made them accessible for the everyday person.

The things outside of us (Circumstances) do *not* create our emotions (Feelings). They merely trigger thoughts. It is our thoughts that create our emotions. It is our emotions that drive our actions. When I heard that, a lot of things clicked into place.

I knew that my size and weight had never been the real problem, I just couldn't figure out what the real problem *was*. I couldn't figure out how to *feel* differently at that weight. Brooke showed me the real source of the hate was my own thinking (the Thoughts), which I *could* change, even if my weight (Circumstance) stayed the same. I had never consciously realized the Thoughts in my mind were optional or that I could actively choose to think differently, but that is exactly what I had been doing during my time with Aphrodite.

In the past, I had only addressed the action of disordered eating using willpower. I never addressed the Thoughts that were driving the disorder in the first place. With my WWAD method, I was accessing the Thoughts first, letting the loving feelings follow, and taking action from a place of love. This is how I ended up truly loving myself as a result.

3. Being

I also love the work of Zig Ziglar. He teaches that we need to "Be" before we can "Do," and we need to "Do" before we can "Have" (BE-DO-HAVE). I had been waiting for self-love to happen in a different order. I thought it would be: HAVE-BE-DO. I kept waiting for the day I simply *did* love myself. I figured, once I did, then I would be loving in my own mind and would treat myself lovingly. The problem was that I was never going to get there with that line of thinking. I had to first focus on BEING. Being is all about how we think and feel within ourselves. That was where I started as I spent time hanging out with my imaginary Aphrodite. I put myself in the headspace and heartspace of someone who already had what I wanted—a loving relationship with herself and her body. I *was* her within myself and in my own mind first. Then, I moved onto DOing—acting in loving ways towards myself. In the end, I genuinely loved myself. This HAVE-ing came last.

4. Bridge Thoughts, Ladder Thoughts, and Neutral Statements

If you've done anything in the world of self-help or personal development, you have probably heard of affirmations. These are positive "I am" statements. I LOVE affirmations. But, sometimes, affirmations *don't* work. If the jump from the current thought to the affirmation is so far that the brain cannot get on board, it can do more damage than good. The brain will spend all its time giving you evidence for why it *isn't* true.

At the beginning of this journey, one of my thoughts was: I hate my body.

I wanted to get to: I love my body.

That was *way* too far of a jump. Repeating "I love myself," or "I love my body," was inconceivable to my brain. It couldn't make that jump. So initially, I thought that affirmations didn't work for me and abandoned them.

When I chose a neutral statement—I have a body—I was creating a bridge (or a ladder) that I could build off of. Not only did this neutral statement take all the emotional charge out of things, it got me half-way to where I was going. I was then able to take a small step to appreciation. And from appreciation, to care. And from care I was able to move to love.

Years later I heard my coach, Brooke Castillo, teach on how to use bridge thoughts and ladder thoughts and realized that was what I had done without knowing it.

If you're struggling with affirmations, see if you can find a neutral thought instead. Or just a slightly better thought. Then, once that one is your truth, take another step.

Some of my favorite neutral statements include:

I have a body.

I am me.

This is.

That happened.

5. Future Focus

I don't know of any single person to whom I should attribute this teaching, because now that I'm aware of it, I find it everywhere.

Tony Robbins says, "If you do what you've always done, you'll get what you've always gotten."

Werner Erhard says, "Create your future from your future not your past."

My coach, Brooke Castillo, tells all of her students in many different ways: if you keep thinking what you have always thought, you will keep creating what you have always created.

The key is to focus on the future, the place you are going. That is what I did in my work with Aphrodite.

I didn't think like a woman who was learning to love herself. I began thinking like I already *did* love myself. I used Aphrodite as a reference point, but I was doing the same work. I was imagining a woman who *already* loved herself rather than trying to figure out the steps *to* love myself. Then I stepped into the future I had created in my mind. I made something new.

Even though I understand it all now in reverse, I *still* think that finding genuine self-love is a miracle of epic proportions. I never *ever* thought this would be possible for me.

I have shared my WWAD method with only a handful of people. Yet, I really felt this story needed to be shared. It is an unconventional method for sure, but it works. I wonder if you might find transformation and growth using this method too.

At the beginning, I was so low, so deep into the darkness of self-loathing, that I don't think I could have done the work of imagining myself acting lovingly. I'm not sure I could have done visualization or the work of Being with me as the star. I couldn't even *imagine* a future where I loved myself. It was a preposterous, fantastical notion. If someone had asked me to do those things, I am pretty sure I would have resisted. Loving myself felt completely out of the question since I did not see myself as lovable.

Getting out of my own head space and imagining someone else being loving allowed me to access an inner wisdom I didn't even know was there. It allowed me to bypass all the reasons I didn't think I deserved it and just start doing it.

The truth is, you don't need to rely on Aphrodite any more than I did.

You are valuable.

You are worthy.

You are lovable.

You are beautiful.

Your body is a good body.

You are enough.

No matter where you are in the journey, *you can* choose to love yourself and your body.

You can choose to think in loving ways.

You can choose to accept everything about yourself.

You can choose to do the loving thing.

You can care for every part of you.

You can completely remove the conditions you've placed on your love and decide it will always be the unconditional kind.

You totally can.

Self-Love is a choice.

But, if that feels a long way off for you, consider asking Aphrodite along for the ride. In every situation, simply ask, *What Would Aphrodite Do?* See if you can figure out what someone who genuinely loves herself, just as she is, would do...even if the person you imagine isn't you. Then, go do that thing. (And don't forget to include, "What Would Aphrodite Think?" and "What Would Aphrodite Feel?" to the equation.)

You've got this.

Now, go unleash your inner Aphrodite.

She's been waiting inside you this whole time.

Epilogue

Who I am Today

June 12, 2019

It has been nearly three and a half years since the trip to the Getty that started me on this journey. So much has happened. So much has changed. Today, we're going back to revisit where this all began. My daughters are now 9 and 12 and just started their summer break. They have changed so much. Unlike our first trip to the museum, both of my girls are old enough to be truly aware of their bodies and themselves and I am grateful everyday that, as of now, the shifts I made with Aphrodite "worked" in terms of what I wanted for my girls. My elder daughter's body is changing, but she is completely comfortable with the process and we have open discussions about what it means to love our body through all the stages. I can't guarantee how that will go for the rest of her life, because I know she will be exposed to more and more voices. I do feel confident that I have been a positive voice and have shown up for my girls the way I wanted to.

They are not the only ones who have changed. I feel so entirely transformed from our last trip. It feels like it has been decades rather than years. Physically, I look about the same. Same height, similar weight—though a little bit heavier. I've got a new haircut and my fashion has evolved, but same face—

maybe with a few additional wrinkles and grey hairs. My health has improved a ton in the last few years. I have way more energy and stamina. After this time at the Getty, I will need hours to recover rather than days. I feel stronger in body and soul.

As we walk into the main building, I catch sight of my reflection in the glass. I look happy and confident. I *am* happy and confident. I stand tall with my head up and my eyes alert. I like my clothes—they've been described as casual with a little bit of sexy—and I think it really works for me. I think I dress like someone who loves herself and her body.

More than the outward appearance, I like the person I see. I'm so proud of the work I've done, so proud of how far I've come. It was hard work, but now I know I can do hard things.

We head for the outdoor gardens first. As we peer over the railing to the gardens below, we are excited to see that they are open this time and we are free to explore them. It is a gorgeous, sunny day, albeit a little warm. As I stroll along the path, sun warming my shoulders, I can't help but get introspective about the parallels. During my first trip, both the garden and I were closed down and closed off. There was so much of myself that I didn't know and hadn't explored, including my capacity to love. More of me is open these days and I'm thankful the gardens are too, because they are lovely! Being in nature and around living, green things is a simple pleasure, but one our family prioritizes.

Back in the museum, my eyes are once again drawn to the other women I see. I look at body shapes. I look at clothes. I look at shoes and handbags. I look at faces. But not to compare myself to them like I used to. I just love seeing all the ways that a person can be lovely. *Wow, she's stunning! Those are amazing shoes. What fantastic style! That haircut is the cutest.*

Moving into a place of unconditional love for myself and my body had nothing to do with comparison. It doesn't even have to do with other people. It is a choice that I made for myself alone. Yet, I have also found it allows me to freely give that same love to others. I sometimes see people who do not seem to be in a place of great health or happiness, reflected in weight or mood, but I don't feel judgement. I feel compassion. I feel love. *I know how hard that is. I've been there.*

I walk around the museum with all the other humans knowing we are all more alike than different. We've all got our struggles. And we're all still valuable and perfectly lovable. I hope for good things for them. I don't want to be thinner than them so I can feel good. I *already* feel good and I want them to feel good too.

At one point we pass a little coffee stand. It smells amazing. The smell of flavored syrup reaches my nose and reminds me of days gone by. There are also all kinds of pastries present that are gorgeous to my eye and would no doubt taste good. I have no desire to have either of those things. Eating something like that would give me a buzz for a bit, then would completely tank my energy later. I would be moody and might get grumpy with the family and spoil our lovely day. I might even have to go home early with an upset stomach. *No thanks! I'll pass.*

As we walk around, I start to feel some hunger. My thought? *No big deal. I'll eat whenever the family decides to.* I've learned that true physical hunger comes and goes. There isn't a rush and it doesn't distract me or keep me from enjoying the art. I keep walking around. I'm aware of the hunger and have plans to nourish my body whenever we stop to eat. Until then, I'm perfectly fine.

As we walk through each room, I feel my anticipation growing. I can't remember exactly where the room of statues is, but I am eager to get there. It's like a long awaited reunion with a dear, dear friend. We've been talking about visiting ever since I finished the first draft of this book.

A friendly museum security guard with a love for kids starts a conversation. I make eye contact, smile, and have a wonderful conversation with him. I never would have done that in the past. I used to be convinced people wouldn't like me or that if I opened my mouth whatever came out would be awkward and embarrassing. Now, I think I'm pretty likable. I enjoy interacting with others and offering some positivity and love to them, since, these days, I've got some to spare. The more I give, the more I seem to get back. The guy tells us some fun and interesting facts we never would have known. We thank him and continue on.

We round a corner and meet a room of white marble. Is this the room? I eagerly scan the pieces. I don't want to skip them, but I really just want to get to *her*.

Suddenly, there she is. I spot her across the room and before I know it, find myself standing right where I was three and a half years ago.

As I stand there, looking at her, I feel such a profound sense of gratitude: for the artist who made the sculpture, for the sentence that ran through my mind as I stood in this exact spot in January of 2016, for the choices I made along the way, for the genuine love I gained. I know she isn't a real person, but we've spent so much time together that she feels like family. If this were a movie, she would wink at me. It's not though. I'm in my real life where she is me, so I give myself a little inner wink to say, we did it!

This time, my husband also gazes at her. He holds my hand and smiles at me while I take in this moment, fully understanding my journey after reading the first draft of this book (and all the subsequent drafts along the way).

Then, when I've had my fill, I continue on with the tour. This time I leave her not with curiosity and hope of a journey beginning, but with the peace and contentment of a journey concluded. While I will always be in the process of growing and becoming, I'm no longer waiting for some future day when I'll love myself. It is true right now.

I *am* a woman who loves and accepts her body.

I *am* a woman who loves and accepts herself.

So…WWAD now? I think she would go and embrace every part of this crazy, messy, wonderful, beautiful, and sometimes painful life.

And I fully intend to.

Appendix

Lessons from Aphrodite:

1. Aphrodite is present for her life.

2. Aphrodite views hunger as neutral.

3. Aphrodite responds to hunger calmly

4. Aphrodite chooses nourishing foods to eat.

5. Aphrodite eats as an act of love.

6. Aphrodite stops eating when she is satisfied.

7. Aphrodite doesn't put harmful things into her body.

8. Aphrodite finds joy outside of food.

9. Aphrodite moves her body in loving ways.

10. Aphrodite responds to her body's signals.

    1. (Expanded) Aphrodite responds to ALL of her body's signals from a place of unconditional love, regardless of their origin.

11. Aphrodite loves her body unconditionally.

Self-Love Lessons:

1. Self-Love takes practice.

2. Self-Love begins with self-knowledge.

3. Self-Love requires ownership.

4. Self-Love follows self-acceptance.

5. Self-Love is available right now.

6. Self-Love speaks kindly.

7. Self-Love leads to authenticity.

8. Self-Love is free.

9. Self-Love results in self-care.

10. Self-Love is a choice.

Acknowledgements

I have to start by thanking my husband, Christopher. When I told you I was thinking of writing a book, you said, "You should totally do that." No hesitation. No doubt. Despite living through the absolute darkest of days with me, you *still* believed I could write a book and that I would have something to say. Your unwavering faith gave me the courage to start, the courage to keep going, and the courage to finish. Thank you for the countless hours of listening to me verbally process. Thank you for contributing to every single part of the process of getting this book into print. Thank you for picking up *all* the slack in our family while I wrote: shopping, cleaning, making dinner, driving our kids all over Los Angeles for extra curricular activities, managing homeschool, and generally being an amazing husband and father. Thank you for loving me unconditionally. Thank you for letting me love you the same. Thank you for all the lessons you taught me through your life about self-love and confidence. You're my best friend and one of my favorite humans on the planet. There is no one I would rather spend time with than you.

A huge thanks to the amazingly talented Heather Walters. Thank you from the bottom of my heart for taking time to give me tips on writing before I started. You told me, "All first drafts are shit." If I hadn't known that, I most likely would have stopped long before we got to the editing process. Instead, as I looked at my first draft that needed so much work, I thought, "Yep. This is just how it is for everyone!" And I kept going. Thank you for being one of my early readers and the high praise you sent back. You helped me believe that this book could be more than what I had originally dreamed for it.

To my dearest friend, Amanda Harrison: When I needed someone other than me and my husband to look at the initial draft of this book, you were the only person I wanted to share it with. I trust you so deeply with every part of me and I knew you would be honest *and* gentle, which is exactly what I needed. Thank you for being my safe space. Thank you for your encouragement and belief in me, not just in this project, but in all things. Thank you for all the endless words of affirmation that you have shared with me in person and in written form over the course of our friendship. You added so much to that "pile" on the metaphorical table and helped me believe I was valuable. Thank you for being the hippie to my uptight. Thank you for being you. Thank you for telling me about naked dancing at our New Moon Mastermind Group (and you too Karen!). Thank you for being your own version of Aphrodite and paving the way for my own revolution.

Lynne Patti, thank you for taking on the task of editing this book. Your thoughtful consideration of every chapter made this work a thousand times better (at least!) than it would have been without you. I've said it before and I'll say it again: I do not have words for how much it meant to me having someone editing the book who also believed in the message. Your love for this content was such an encouragement and motivation through the endless hours of editing. Thank you for believing in the project. Thank you for believing in me. Thanks for being willing to figure out our way of editing a book. (Maybe someday we'll ask the rest of the writing community how *they* do it...or maybe not!) Thank you for going on this journey with me and with Aphrodite. Your love for her and your own progress through the book's message helped me really believe that this work could help other women. I love every bit of you.

Thank you Alexis Logsdon for being the kind of person who catches errors that others miss and for using that talent to catch the last few in this book.

A huge thank you to all of my coaching clients. Thank you for trusting me while I was still in process and ironing out my message. You all mean the world to me. I would not be here if it wasn't for your trust in me and the unending stories of your growth and success. You were the evidence I needed to really believe, deep down in the marrow of my bones, that I had something valuable to offer the world. You did the work, but I'm grateful to have been part of the process.

A special shout out to Jenn Harp. You were the very first person who I told about my WWAD method. The way that you immediately connected with it planted the seed for this book. If you hadn't been so all-in for trying it out, I might never have seen it's worth for others. It has been a privilege to watch your process of "becoming."

And, finally, a huge thank you to my daughters, Zoe and Nadia (who will not be allowed to read this until they are older). I did not love myself enough to do this work for me, but I loved you enough to do it for you. Thank you for being the cutest *why* anyone could ask for. Thank you for being flexible when I worked late. Thank you for being gracious when I was still writing chapters in my head after my computer was closed and was totally not present while you told me about your day. Thank you for not complaining (too much) when we had the same meals over and over because all of my creativity was going into this project. Thank you for teaching me the meaning of unconditional love. I love everything about who you were, who you are, and who you are becoming. And I always will. No matter what.

Are you ready for your own self-love revolution?

Continue the journey at:

www.LorrieGray.com

Made in the USA
Middletown, DE
17 November 2019

78857287R00159